D0543046

Discovering Glasgow

Discovering Glasgow

WILLIAM W. BARR

The Molendinar Press

The Molendinar Press Ltd.
16 Laurel Street
Glasgow G11 7QR
Scotland

First Published by The Molendinar Press 1980

Copyright © William W. Barr 1980

ISBN 0 904002 53 5

Made and Printed in Great Britain by
William Collins Sons & Co. Ltd., Glasgow

To

HEWIT GRAHAM
Secretary of the Springburn Association

in recognition of his many services
to Springburn and his native
City of Glasgow

CONTENTS

Foreword

Routes

Appendix

Origins of Glasgow Streets

FOREWORD

Foreword by the ex-Lord Provost, David Hodge, CBE, OStJ, JP, LLD.

Glasgow is a city which inspires its citizens with fanatical loyalty and constantly surprises visitors with the splendour of its buildings and parks. In the 18th Century, travellers were charmed by its spacious streets and elegant houses; a century later they were impressed by its confidence as one of the power houses of the industrial revolution. Today they are often misled by the surface mess of urban renewal to discover the city's heritage.

William Barr's excellent 'Discovering Glasgow', written in his easy style, takes visitor and native alike through the city, bringing alive the buildings and the men who built them or dwelt within their walls.

This new publication nicely enhances the rich volume of books touching every aspect of life in our city and for this reason I have much pleasure in commending it.

David Hodge

Discovering Glasgow

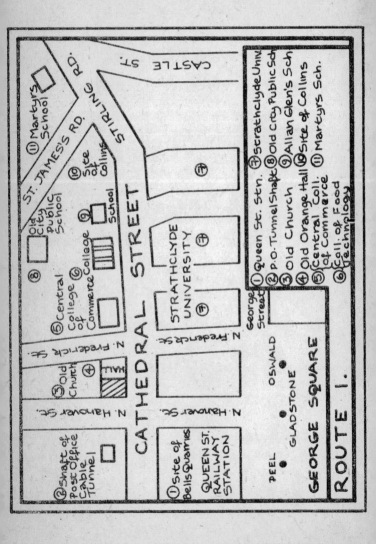

ROUTE 1.

1. Site of Bells Quarries
2. Shaft of Post Office Cable Tunnel
3. Old Church
4. Old Orange Hall
5. Central Coll. of Commerce
6. Coll. of Food Technology
7. Queen St. Stn.
8. P.O. Tunnel Shaft
9. Old Church
10. Site of Collins
11. Central Coll. of Commerce

1. Queen St. Stn.
2. P.O. Tunnel Shaft
3. Old Church
4. Old Orange Hall
5. Central Coll. of Commerce
6. Coll. of Food Technology
7. Strathclyde Univ.
8. Old City Public Sch.
9. Allan Glen's Sch.
10. Site of Collins
11. Martyrs Sch.

Route 1

NORTH HANOVER STREET, CATHEDRAL STREET, STIRLING ROAD

Where can we find a better place to start a ramble through Glasgow, than North Hanover Street, running beside Queen Street Railway Station, and abutting on beautiful George Square, at one time said to be the finest square in Europe?

A notable family, the Bells of Cowcaddens, owned quarries where now the Queen Street Station stands. They also owned Bell's Pottery, and many pieces of discarded pottery were found when the foundations of the S.M.T. (Scottish Midland Transport) offices were built in Killermont Street, in 1974, on the site of an infilled quarry. Many of these pieces are valued by collectors, and a number are on show in the People's Palace, Glasgow Green.

The firm of J. & M. P. Bell was founded in 1842 and situated between Port Dundas and St Rollox. Once the biggest pottery in Scotland, its products are still prized by Scottish collectors.

We slowly climb the steep incline of North Hanover Street and turn right into Cathedral Street which as its name implies, leads to Glasgow Cathedral.

On our right are the extensive buildings of the Strathclyde University, the city's second university, which at one time was known as Glasgow Technical College.

On our left at the corner of North Hanover Street and Cathedral Street, there is a vacant piece of ground on which at one time stood a building numbered 400 Cathedral Street. It used to be the Headquarters of the Post Office Engineering Department in Glasgow. On this site now stands the shaft of the Post Office Cable tunnel that carries cables from the post office cable chambers in Dial House in Bothwell Street. At the opposite corner, in Cathedral Street, are the premises of McDonald's Furniture Stores where the Church of New Jerusalem used to be. This church followed the teachings of Emanuel Swedenborg (1688–1772), scientist, philosopher and mystic.

Next door is a red sandstone building which, until a few years ago, was the Headquarters of the Orange Lodge in Glasgow. It was later taken over on a temporary basis by the Apostolic Church when their church at 50 North Frederick Street was demolished and now belongs to the District Council which intends to landscape North Frederick Street.

At 300 Cathedral Street we pass the Central College of Commerce opened on 24th May, 1963. This building won a Civic Trust Award, as stated on a plaque on the wall outside its main entrance. Also at No. 230 are the three modern blocks of The Glasgow College of Food Technology, built on the site of Grafton Square in 1973. It is the first college of its kind in Scotland to be entirely concerned with food.

Continuing along Cathedral Street we reach Allan Glen's School which was first started in 1853 in a building at the south-east corner of North Hanover Street. It was there that Charles Rennie Mackintosh, the world-renowned Glasgow architect, was educated. Nearby, at 201 St James' Road is the City Public School, built in 1906, and now used as an extension for Allan Glen's School. There is a plaque in the gymnasium that states John McLaren Biggar (1874–1943), a pupil of City Public School, was a former Provost of the City of Glasgow.

Cut in large letters in the stone wall of a tenement building at 168 Cathedral Street, there used to be the inscription 'Provanside', signifying that this was once the ancient lands of Provanside. This building was demolished in 1978. Across from where it once stood is the Stenhouse Building given to Strathclyde University by Hugh Stenhouse in memory of his father and opened in 1972.

Further east is a building that originally belonged to Collins, the famous publishing house that was founded in 1819 and made its publishing debut with *The Christian and Civic Economy of Large Towns* by Thomas Chalmers.

We now pass along Stirling Road, and to our left we observe in Parson Street, St Mungo's Roman Catholic Church with a square tower still awaiting a spire. It has three carved heads above the archway of the entrance and although it is difficult to establish who they represent, there is little doubt that one is St Mungo. It is one of the oldest Catholic churches in Glasgow: the foundation stone was laid in 1866.

Next to it is the red sandstone Martyrs' Public School, designed in 1895 by Charles Rennie Mackintosh. This school was at one time threatened with demolition, but so highly thought of is the work of Mackintosh that protests came from as far afield as the Louvre Museum in Paris to save the school. At one time the Martyrs' School was under the jurisdiction of Martyrs' Parish Church, Monkland Street. The name Martyr was given in memory of Jerome Russell and John Kennedy, martyrs who were burned to death during the Reformation.

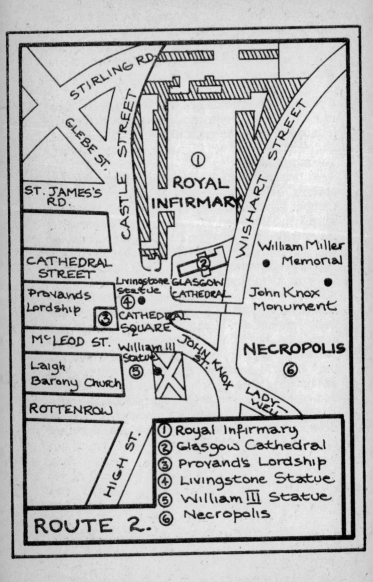

STIRLING RD.

GLEBE ST.

CASTLE STREET

ST. JAMES'S RD.

① ROYAL INFIRMARY

WISHART STREET

William Miller Memorial

CATHEDRAL STREET

Livingstone Statue

GLASGOW CATHEDRAL ②

John Knox Monument

Provands Lordship

④

③

CATHEDRAL SQUARE

McLEOD ST.

William III Statue

NECROPOLIS

Laigh Barony Church

⑤

JOHN KNOX ST.

⑥

ROTTENROW

LADY WELL

HIGH ST.

① Royal Infirmary
② Glasgow Cathedral
③ Provand's Lordship
④ Livingstone Statue
⑤ William III Statue
⑥ Necropolis

ROUTE 2.

Route 2

CASTLE STREET, CATHEDRAL SQUARE

Ahead of us in Castle Street is the massive structure of the Royal Infirmary designed by James Miller. The foundation stone was laid by the Prince of Wales, later King George V in 1907, and in the same year the foundation stone was laid for the Mitchell Library by Andrew Carnegie. The first Royal Infirmary had been opened in 1792 and the foundation stone of the third Royal Infirmary was laid in 1974 by Simpson Stevenson, Chairman of the Western Regional Hospital Board.

As we proceed down Castle Street there is a large marble plaque on the wall of the Royal Infirmary to the memory of Lord Lister (1827–1912) who originated the use of antiseptics which he practiced in the famous Ward Number 24 of the Royal Infirmary.

The crest of the Royal Infirmary consists of a three-headed Scottish Thistle with the stem of the thistle entwined with the Serpent of Aesculapius, and inscribed with the motto *Auspice Caelo*, meaning 'Favoured by Heaven'.

At the corner of Cathedral Street and Castle Street stood the Barony Free Church, built in 1867. The 120 foot tower was for long a noted landmark. The purchase of the ground and building of the church was largely financed by the Burns family, of the present Burns and Laird Lines Ltd., Shipowners. The site was bought for £3,000, but in 1973 the church had to be demolished owing to damage done by the nearby Post Office tunnel. Dwelling houses attached to the church in High Street still stand, but may be demolished in the 1980's.

Soon we turn left into Cathedral Square and pause here for a while to look at the many items of interest, because we are now in the heart of old Glasgow. Beside us is the beautiful Gothic edifice of Glasgow Cathedral founded by St Mungo in 543, on ground consecrated at an earlier date by St Ninian. It is the only pre-Reformation church in Glasgow, contains priceless works of art and is one of Glasgow's chief tourist attractions. Unfortunately in 1846 the north-west tower and the consistory tower were demolished and many hundred-weights of old documents were consigned to the flames.

Archbishop Beaton was the last Roman Catholic Archbishop to reside in the Bishop's Palace before the Reformation in 1560. This building, also known as 'Glasgow Castle', was in Cathedral Square. Its site is now marked by a white stone directly in front of the Royal Infirmary.

The Archbishop fled to France and left all his possessions, including many of the treasures of Glasgow Cathedral, to the Scots College, Rue Cardinal Lemoine, Paris. Indeed he is commonly regarded as the second founder of the college which had originally been set up by David, Bishop of Moray. The treasures, however, were later lost, and the Scots College has not been used as a college since the French Revolution. Beaton himself is buried in the Church of St Jean de Lateran in Rome. On his tomb is the following inscription.

SACRATUS ROMA 1552
OBIIT 24 APRIL 1603
AETATIS SUAE 86

Also above the tomb are 16 lines of Latin Verse.

Directly opposite the Cathedral is Provands Lordship, the oldest house in Glasgow. It is generally accepted that it was built in 1471 by Bishop Andrew

Muirhead, but an old postcard exists which states that it dates from 1455. This postcard was bought from B. Innes's confectionery which at that time shared the ground floor of Provands Lordship with a fruit shop, a barber shop and a salesroom. The latter, however, a lean-to at the south end of the building, has long since been demolished.

Mary Queen of Scots probably lived in this house in 1566, and the Casket Letters may have been written here. She was later executed in 1587 at Fotheringay Castle, mainly on the evidence of these letters.

At one time one of the ports of Glasgow was beside the Castle and designated the Castle Yett Port.

In Cathedral Square we have many statues including one of David Livingstone, the African Missionary and explorer, who was born at Lower Blantyre in 1813 and was buried in Westminster Abbey in 1873.

Within the Gardens of the Royal Infirmary is the statue of James Lumsden, Lord Provost of Glasgow from 1843 to 1847, and treasurer of the Royal Infirmary. At each side of the entrance to the Glasgow Necropolis which leads off Cathedral Square is a statue. The one on the left is erected to the memory of James White of Overtown, a great benefactor to religious organizations, and the statue to the right is of James Arthur, the founder of Arthur & Co., the well known Glasgow firm in Miller Street, and incidentally, the only firm in the centre of the city to be bombed during the last war, in 1945.

Situated in Cathedral Square and facing the Leaigh Barony Church is the statue of the Reverend Norman MacLeod, D.D. (1812–1872) with a Bible in his hand. He was a prominent minister of the church.

The only equestrian statue in the square and the oldest statue of this kind in Glasgow is that of King William III, Prince of Orange. The statue was gifted in 1735 by James MacRae, a poor Ayrshire boy who ran away to sea and eventually became a Governor of Madras. For around 200 years the statue stood previously in the Trongate.

According to Robert L. Ripley, in his series, *Believe It or Not*, King William III was nicknamed 'Wee Willie Winkie' in many Jacobite songs.

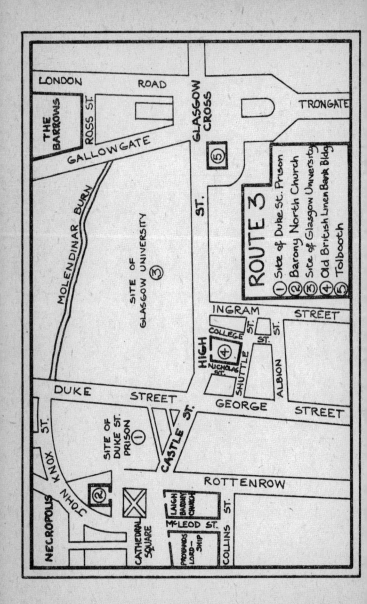

ROUTE 3

① Site of Duke St. Prison
② Barony North Church
③ Site of Glasgow University
④ Old British Linen Bank Bldg.
⑤ Tolbooth

12

Route 3

HIGH STREET – GLASGOW CROSS

Leaving Cathedral Square, we travel down High Street, past the Ladywell Housing Estate, called after the medieval well in nearby Ladywell Street, and built on the site of the grim Duke Street Prison.

It was in this prison that Susan Newell, the last woman to be hanged in Scotland, was hanged in 1923.

Associated with Duke Street Prison was the Glasgow Discharged Prisoners Aid Society which occupied a building in Cathedral Street that now belongs to Glasgow Cathedral and helped more than 405,000 ex-prisoners in the course of a hundred years.

Here we pass Rottenrow, the route of the kings and one of Glasgow's oldest streets. There is a newspaper advertisement from 1780 that speaks of 'Summer quarters to be let at West end of Rottenrow': proof, if proof were needed, that Glasgow was once a rural town.

At 195 High Street, now a vacant site, stood the old hydraulic pumping station built in 1893–1895. Built in red sandstone and as attractive as a castle, this fine piece of industrial Glasgow was demolished in 1973.

Near the Ladywell is the Barony North Church at 18 Cathedral Square, a beautiful Gothic structure built in 1889 and the only church in Glasgow featuring collectively, the life-sized statues of the apostles Matthew, Mark, Luke and John and also the Saints Peter and Paul.

The incline of High Street down to Duke Street was known as the 'Bell O' the Brae'. It was here Sir William Wallace defeated an English force in 1297. At this point on each side of the road are beautiful red sandstone tenements which may be demolished to make way for the future east flank of the Ring Road.

We now cross Duke Street and still proceed down High Street. On our left on the site of the College Goods Station there stood at one time the Glasgow College or University and the Hunterian Museum, Blackfriars Church, the Botanical Gardens and the Infantry Barracks at Gallowgate. These buildings were all removed in 1870 to make way for the huge railway yards. Facing College Street, on High Street, is a plaque indicating that this was the gateway to the Glasgow University founded in 1451.

At the corner of High Street and Nicholas Street there is a plaque on the wall of the old British Linen Bank stating that the poet Thomas Campbell lived in a house on this site from 1777 till 1844. The one-time British Linen Bank is surmounted by a statue of Pallas, Goddess of Wisdom and Weaving, and a representation of Pallas was used as a seal for the Bank's transactions. Above the Bank's door is a stained glass window of a flax ship which indicates a connection with the Bank's flax and linen trade. The shop premises at the north corner of College Street and High Street are all that now remain of the two tenements that stood at each side of College Street. These were designed by James Adam and are said to have been occupied by the High Street college professors. The poet William Motherwell, who was editor of the *Glasgow Courier,* one of the city's earliest newspapers, was born in the southern tenement. Before the buildings were demolished in 1973 it was suggested that one building at least should be used as a closed theatre or even as an extension to Glasgow University, but these ideas conflicted with the proposal to carry the Ring Road through the site.

Soon we pass Blackfriars Street, so called because this was once the old highway to the wealthy Blackfriars Monastery that stood in the College Goods

Station. In 1699, a new church was built on the site of the old Monastery Church. When this church and the surrounding ground were taken by the South Western Railway Company, the church was demolished and rebuilt in Westercraigs where it still stands. The 17th century chapel bell was for twenty years in Westercraigs, but when the University chapel was built in Gilmorehill it was transferred there.

Further down we come to McPherson Street which takes its name from the McPherson coat of arms that first stood on a house belonging to John McPherson of Blantyre and was then incorporated into the wall of the present street when that house was demolished.

Nearby is the Mercat Cross surmounted with the unicorn, a common symbol in Scotland. For example, the Royal Arms of Scotland are supported by two unicorns. As far back as 1175 there was a market on the site of the Mercat Cross and Glasgow Cross Railway Station, which originally formed part of the Caledonian Railway System, stood here as well until it was finally demolished on 9th August, 1977.

It is on record that in 1873 the area around the corner of Gallowgate and High Street was a very prosperous commercial area and was known as the 'Golden Acre'. It was said that no merchant ever failed that had a business in this select area.

A marker stone in front of the Tolbooth indicated that the gallows once stood here, but it has since been covered up with tarmacadam during street renovations in 1977.

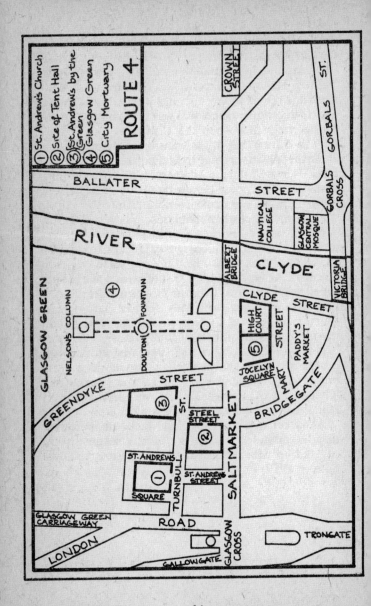

ROUTE 4.

① St. Andrew's Church
② Site of Tent Hall
③ St. Andrews by the Green
④ Glasgow Green
⑤ City Mortuary

Route 4

SALTMARKET – ST ANDREW'S STREET TURNBULL STREET – GREENDYKE STREET – SALTMARKET

We now travel down the Saltmarket that was once the site of a market selling salt for curing salmon and herring, and we turn left into St Andrew's Street where Glasgow Police Headquarters stood before being removed to Pitt Street in 1975.

Attached to the wall of the 1st floor is a memorial of the 1914–18 war in memory of the 173 men who were killed, and also a memorial to the 35 men killed in the 1939–45 war.

At the end of St Andrew's Street, in Turnbull Street, is St Andrew's Parish Church designed by the Glasgow architect Allan Dreghorn and completed by master mason Mungo Naismith in 1756. The stones to build this church came from the Crackling House Quarry where Queen Street Station now stands, and the church organ (now on view in the People's Palace) was built by James Watt. It was also here that Bonnie Prince Charlie stabled his horses in 1745 while the building was still under construction. St Andrew's Square itself, once the most fashionable part of Glasgow, was built at a much later date.

The famous Tent Hall is also located in Turnbull Street. This was built in 1876 and named after the tent on Glasgow Green which was the headquarters of the Moodie and Sankey Evangelical campaign of 1874. In the 1920's it enjoyed a huge success, attracting audiences of up to 1,000 and providing between 2,000 and 3,000 needy people every week with a free breakfast, and in 1974 Moodie and Sankey were duly commemorated with a Centenary Meeting complete with a Centenary Tent set up on the same spot as the original. Unfortunately, however, the Hall was finally closed in 1979.

Also closed is St Andrew's-by-the-Green Episcopal Church nearby. The oldest Episcopal church in Scotland, this was built in 1751. General Wolfe of Quebec fame and many other soldiers stationed at the old Gallowgate barracks worshipped here, and Doctor Gordon, minister of the church from 1844–1899 and an outstanding social reformer and historian, wrote the *Glasghu Facies*, a popular work about Glasgow. Due to the movement of the population away from the city centre, though, the membership gradually dwindled away and the church had to be shut. The last service was held on Sunday 23rd February, 1975 before a packed congregation, many people having come from miles away not to miss such an occasion.

We continue our journey and turn right into Greendyke Street. On our left is the main entrance to Glasgow Green, where great crowds of people used to gather to witness public executions carried out here between 1814 and 1865. The last large assembly of people to stand here was in 1956. They were awaiting news of the mass murderer Peter Manuel who was later hanged at Barlinnie Prison. Pearlie James Wilson, the Strathaven Weaver, who has a monument erected to his memory on the site of his house in Strathaven, was taken out of his iron prison in the High Court on a hurdle and hanged in front of the High Court in 1820. Dr Pritchard was the last man to be hanged in public outside the High Court in 1865 for poisoning his wife and mother-in-law. There are many stories circulating about Dr Pritchard who was buried in the precincts of the High Court including one to the effect that the fine leather boots he wore at his execution were later recovered from the grave and sold.

At 194 Saltmarket is the City Mortuary which is open 24 hours a day. Here the Chief Mortician and his three colleagues deal with around 1400–1500 sudden deaths in the city each year. Now that the city is in the Strathclyde Region their grim work will be increased.

At this point we turn north up the Saltmarket, which is being cleaned up as part of a rehabilitation scheme. We pass by the Bridgegate which is one of the oldest streets in Glasgow. At one time it was known as the Fishergate as it had been mostly built by fishermen and fish dealers who had formed themselves into a society.

Later it briefly became a very fashionable quarter where wealthy merchants and even the nobility resided and it was here that William Miller, the author of *Wee Willie Winkie*, was born in 1810. He has a memorial in the Glasgow Necropolis but he is actually buried in Tollcross Churchyard.

As we retrace our journey up the Saltmarket we come upon a number of small shops occupying the ground floors of mostly derelict tenements. The shops sell goods ranging from cameras to cut-price clothes. The nearby markets of Glasgow Barrows and Paddy's Market seem to draw people from far and near seeking a bargain in this area.

In spite of the continued exodus of the residents from this quarter, the shops carry on an extremely brisk trade.

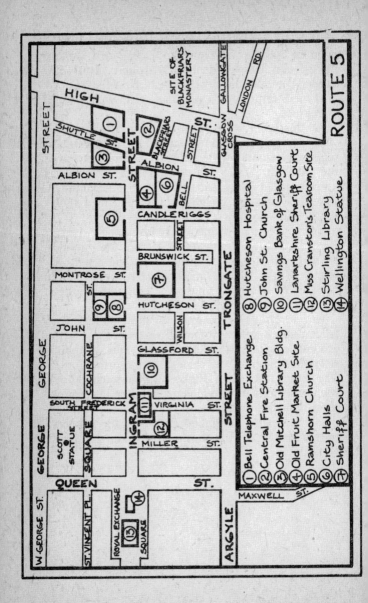

ROUTE 5

Map legend:
1. Bell Telephone Exchange
2. Central Fire Station
3. Old Mitchell Library Bldg.
4. Old Fruit Market Site
5. Ramshorn Church
6. City Halls
7. Sheriff Court
8. Hutcheson Hospital
9. John St. Church
10. Savings Bank of Glasgow
11. Lanarkshire Sheriff Court
12. Miss Cranston's Tearoom Site
13. Stirling Library
14. Wellington Statue

Map labels: HIGH STREET, SHUTTLE ST., ALBION ST., ALBION ST., CANDLERIGGS, MONTROSE ST., JOHN ST., GEORGE ST., GEORGE GEORGE ST., W. GEORGE ST., QUEEN ST., COCHRANE ST., SOUTH FREDERICK STREET, ST. VINCENT PL., ROYAL EXCHANGE SQUARE, SCOTT STATUE, GEORGE SQUARE, BELL STREET, BLACKFRIARS STREET, SITE OF BLACKFRIARS MONASTERY, GLASGOW CROSS, LONDON RD., GALLOWGATE, BRUNSWICK ST., HUTCHESON ST., GLASSFORD ST., VIRGINIA ST., MILLER ST., WILSON ST., INGRAM STREET, TRONGATE, ARGYLE STREET, MAXWELL ST.

20

Route 5

HIGH STREET – INGRAM STREET

We again reach High Street and then turn left into Ingram Street, named after Lord Provost Ingram who was Lord Provost of Glasgow from 1762 to 1763. There is a plaque commemorating him in the Merchants House, 7 West George Street. We pass by the Bell Telephone Exchange at No. 30 Ingram Street, built in 1938. The Royal Crown and G VI R are cut above the door.

Opposite the Bell Telephone Exchnage at 33 Ingram Street is the Central Fire Station built in 1899 with a particularly fine example of the Glasgow Coat of Arms above the main entrance. It is of interest to note that the Glasgow Coat of Arms was granted in 1866 in its present form by the Lord Lyon. Prior to this time the City of Glasgow had no official Coat of Arms. The motto is a shorter version of the original motto which ran *Lord, let Glasgow flourish by the preaching of the Word and praising Thy Name*. Inside the Engine Room a marble plaque has been erected to the memory of the 19 firemen and salvagemen who died on 28th March 1960 in the Cheapside Street Whisky Bond fire. The dog Wallace (1894–1902) of T.V. fame, the famous Fire Service mascot, is preserved and on show in a glass case in the Fire Station.

At the corner of Albion Street and 60 Ingram Street stand the Albion Buildings part of which was at one time used as the Mitchell Library. The Mitchell Library was founded by the tobacco merchant Stephen Mitchell, of Stephen Mitchell and Co. The library was opened by Lord Provost Bain in 1877. Bain Street Calton was named after him.

The Fruit Market was active in this area as well until 1969, when it was removed to a 29-acre site at Blochairn formerly occupied by a steelworks. It still retains Bell telephone numbers and is destined to become the largest covered market in Britain. The north side of the old market, which had the stone head of a bullock over the entrance, suggesting that it may also have been a meat market at one time, was demolished in 1978, but the rest of the glass-covered structure survives in all its old world charm, and the names of the fruit dealers can still be seen beside the derelict fruit stalls inside. The highly successful Clydefair International Bazaar was held here in June 1973.

It can be seen when passing through this area that many of the premises in the adjoining streets were once used as extensions of the old Fruit Market. It was this overcrowding that finally led to a change of location.

Facing down Candleriggs is the Ramshorn Church that takes its name from the Ramshorn estate on which it was built in 1824. It replaced a former church built in 1724. On the pavement directly in front of the church is a cross with the letters R.F. and A.F., the initials of the Foulis Brothers, early printers in Glasgow and founders of the Glasgow Academy of Fine Arts.

The churchyard is also the burial place of Emile L'Angelier who was thought to have been poisoned by cocoa laced with arsenic from the hand of Madeleine Smith. Though probably guilty, she was acquitted by an Edinburgh jury and went on to become one of the most fashionable hostesses in the country. Also buried here is John Anderson who founded the Anderson's Institution which eventually became Strathclyde University. His grandfather was minister of Ramshorn Church in 1720 and he is also buried here. A plaque inside the church indicates this fact. A number of years ago there was, attached to the wall inside the entrance to the Ramshorn Churchyard, an old tombstone indicating the last resting place of members of the family of McAslan, one of the oldest seed merchants in Glasgow, who advertised their wares in the *Glasgow Journal* of 23rd January 1758. There is also a plaque to Sir John Alexander MacDonald (born 1815) who became the first Prime Minister of Canada in 1867. He was born in Brunswick Street, in the same building as The Angus Bar near Argyle Street.

The first pavement in Candleriggs was laid in 1777 on the east side of the street between Bell Street and Trongate. There are many versions of how this street got its name and the most commonly accepted is that it was called after a candleworks that at one time stood here. The Royal Bank of Scotland, at 127 Candleriggs has inside its premises a stone dated 1597 and these words are inscribed on it:

BLISSIT BE YE LORD OUR
GOD FOR ALL HIS GIFTIS
REBUILT 1824

The stone was removed from the building which formerly occupied this site and was placed here in 1939. The building in question is thought to have belonged to the Incorporation of Bakers, one of the 14 old trades of Glasgow. This bank is now closed and the premises are unoccupied.

We now come to a fine building at 137 Ingram Street. This is a historic building built in 1855 which has to be retained. It is the premises of Campbell Stewart & McDonald and is the oldest establishment of its kind in Glasgow. It is interesting to note from the names listed on the war memorials displayed inside the building that 1172 members of the staff served in the 1914–18 war and 304 served in the 1939–45 war.

The original James Campbell of this firm was Lord Provost of the City of Glasgow. His son, also James Campbell, was M.P. for the Glasgow and Aberdeen Universities from 1880 to 1906. Henry Campbell Bannerman, a second son of James Campbell, who was born in Kelvinside, was elected an M.P. and later became Prime Minister of Great Britain in 1906. There is an underground tunnel connecting 137 Ingram Street with 112 Ingram Street. The latter building belonged to Campbell Stewart & McDonald prior to 1938 but was then taken over by the Corporation of Glasgow Health and Welfare Department and now belongs to the Greater Glasgow Health Board.

Next we see the County Buildings containing the Sheriff Court and a number of other courts. Parts of this building were used as the Glasgow City Chambers before the present City Chambers in George Square were opened by Queen Victoria in 1888.

Below in the archives of the Sheriff Courts are old books containing records dating from the eleventh century and embracing old laws and statutes.

These courts are the busiest in Europe, although at one time Bonn, in Germany, held this position. Courts 9 and 10 were once the Merchants Hall, and Paderewski, the renowned pianist, once played there. In the basement there was a whipping room complete with a whipping table and collections of whips which are on show in the Glasgow Police Black Museum in Pitt Street. There are also 24 cells for those awaiting trial and a lady in white is said to haunt the building.

Across the road at 158 Ingram Street is Hutchesons' Hospital with the statues of its two founders, the Hutcheson Brothers Thomas and George. The statues are over 300 years old and were originally in the tower of the former hospital at Trongate.

John Street on the right is the only street in Glasgow adorned with beautiful stone arches and also of interest is the old John Street Church now used as a night shelter for homeless men.

At 177 Ingram Street is the Head Office of the Savings Bank of Glasgow which first started in 1836 in two rented rooms in Hutchesons' Hospital. It is perhaps the only bank in Glasgow to have a life-size statue of St Mungo above the entrance.

Nearby is Lanarkshire House. Now used as an extension of the Sheriff Court, this was originally built as the Union Bank Headquarters in 1840. You can still see the old safe and steel floor.

There are beautiful carved bannisters inside, and eight statues adorn the facade which are said to represent Justice with a sword, Britannia and the Muses.

One of Miss Cranston's famous tearooms designed by Mackintosh once stood at the corner of Ingram Street and Miller Street. Ironically, this later became Alston's Tearoom where you could get a cup of tea for an old penny, and the site is now occupied by the Ingram Hotel which has a suite named after Mackintosh.

Miller Street itself was where many of the leading merchants and tobacco lords lived around 1780.

At the end of Ingram Street we come to Stirling's Library. This building was originally built as a town mansion for William Cunningham of Lainshaw in 1780 by Madeleine Smith's grandfather and at that time was supposed to be the most elite dwelling in the west of Scotland. Later converted into the Royal Exchange, it was visited by such distinguished figures as Louis Bonaparte, Gladstone and Dickens, and finally, for a while, the National Telephone Company had its headquarters here until it was taken over by the government in 1907.

Directly in front of Stirling's Library is the equestrian statue of Wellington, who won the decisive Battle of Waterloo in 1815. The statue was designed by Baron Marochetti of Turin in Italy and the horse is considered one of his masterpieces. Bronze panels on the sides of the base of the statue depict incidents from the time of Waterloo. Opposite here at 110 Queen Street was formerly the British Linen Bank, the first building in Glasgow to be built to the metric scale. It now belongs to the Bank of Scotland which merged with the British Linen Bank in 1971.

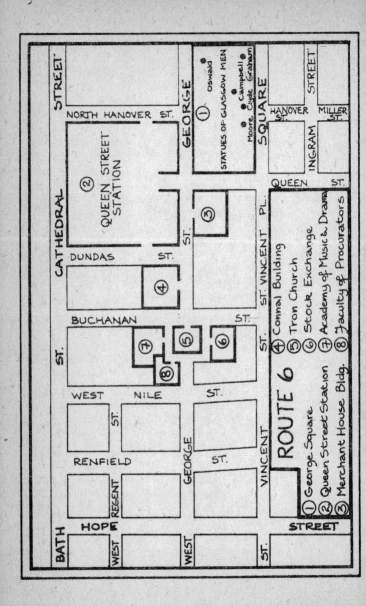

STREET

GEORGE STREET

① Oswald
● Campbell
● Clyde ● Graham
● Moore

STATUES OF GLASGOW MEN

SQUARE

HANOVER ST.   MILLER STREET

NORTH HANOVER ST.

② QUEEN STREET STATION

CATHEDRAL

QUEEN   ST.

INGRAM

③

DUNDAS   ST.

④

ST. VINCENT PL.

BUCHANAN   ST.

⑦   ⑤   ⑥

⑧

ST.

WEST   NILE   ST.

RENFIELD   GEORGE   ST.

REGENT

BATH   HOPE   STREET

WEST   WEST

VINCENT   ST.

ROUTE 6

① George Square
② Queen Street Station
③ Merchant House Bldg.
④ Connal Building
⑤ Tron Church
⑥ Stock Exchange
⑦ Academy of Music & Drama
⑧ Faculty of Procurators

28

Route 6

QUEEN STREET – WEST GEORGE STREET – ST GEORGE'S PLACE – WEST GEORGE STREET

We now turn into Queen Street. This was laid down in 1777 and originally called Cow Loan before being re-named after Queen Charlotte, wife of George III and grandmother of Queen Victoria. Charlotte Street is also named after her and George Square is named after George III.

Skirting beautiful George Square, which contains 12 statues, many of them representing Glasgow men, we turn left into West George Street. On our right is the Queen Street Railway Station which serves all stations in Scotland north of the River Clyde. The station is built on the site of the Crackling House Quarry and originally served the Edinburgh and Glasgow Railway Company.

A nearby church which had long been used as offices by the railway staff was demolished in 1975. It had been built in 1819. The first minister was Ralph Wardlaw, a famous preacher of his day. The classic design of the building was admired by Queen Victoria when she visited Glasgow in 1849. The old pulpit from this church was later taken to Elgin Place Congregational Church, now derelict. David Livingstone, the African missionary and explorer, studied theology under Wardlaw and was also a member of this church. Consort House now stands on its site at 12 West George Street.

At the corner of George Square and West George Street is the Merchants House Building and also housed in this building is the Chamber of Commerce, founded in 1873, the oldest in the world and at one time the largest. There are on show many fine exhibits relating to the Merchants House and the Chamber of Commerce. One example is the more-than-life-size statue of Kirkman Finlay (1773–1842) of Castle Toward, the notable Glasgow Merchant and M.P., and Lord Provost of the city in 1812. His house was in Queen Street.

We now pass by Dundas Street which perpetuates the name of Lord Dundas who cut the first sod for the building of the Forth and Clyde Canal. Port Dundas is also called after him.

In Dundas Place there used to be a plaque indicating that the famous Thorn Tree Tearoom had been there. Dundas Place no longer exists, but this plaque has been preserved together with a milestone from Dundas Street on which are the words 'Carmunnock 6 miles and Cambuslang 4 miles'.

At 34 West George Street is a very artistically designed building. It is almost a copy of the Ritter in Heidelberg, Germany. William Connal of Connal & Co., Warehousekeepers, built it in 1900 from Dumfriesshire red sandstone and Scottish granite. The sculptured heads of J. B. Neilson, inventor of the hot blast, James Watt, inventor of the steam engine, Dixon of Dixon's Iron Works, and Baird the iron master adorn the facade of the building.

Approaching Buchanan Street we come to St George's Tron Church completed in 1808. Then it was considered to be situated too far out in the country from Glasgow, for even at that time the ground on which nearby West Nile Street now stands, was well known as providing good coverts for hare shooting.

Inside the entrance to St George's Tron Church, fixed on the wall, is a Roll of Honour inscribed with the names of 312 men, and one nurse, who served in the 1914–18 war. There is also a tastefully carved wooden memorial to the 36 men killed in the Second

World War. There is also a further war memorial in grateful memory of Cleweth T. L. Donaldson and 78 employees of the Donaldson Line Limited, who gave their lives for King and Country in the 1914–18 war.

The Rev. Tom Allan, who died in 1965, was a noted minister of St George's Tron. He opened, in 1962, the Rehabilitation Centre at 23 Elmbank Street, Glasgow, as a centre for hospitality and spiritual help to alcoholics, drug addicts and outcasts. In 1969 the Centre was renamed the Tom Allan Centre in his memory.

We now cross Buchanan Street, which dates from 1770, and enter St George's Place, skirting the side of the Glasgow Stock Exchange, which was founded in 1844, and built in the Venetian Gothic style. Its first wing was added in 1875.

Over to the north side of St George's Place is the Royal Scottish Academy of Music and Drama and on the facade of the building are sculptured figures representing Reynolds the painter, Wren the architect, Purcell the composer, and Flaxman the sculptor and architect. There are also two groups of figures representing literature and science. These figures were all cut from models by John Mossman.

At the corner of St George's Place and West Nile Street there stands the building of the Royal Faculty of Procurators. It was designed by Charles Wilson, one of the most important architects of his day. The building has been described as the smallest but most richly finished example of the Venetian phase of Glasgow architecture.

Adorning the keystones of the 14 arched basement windows are 14 clearly cut masks representing well known personalities connected with the legal profession. They were designed by Mr Handyside Ritchie of Edinburgh, and by Mr Shanks of Parliamentary Road, Glasgow.

Among the notable lawyers depicted is Forbes of Culloden who was Lord President of the Court of Session. He tried to persuade Lord Lovat not to assist Bonnie Prince Charlie in the 1745 rebellion. Forbes raised a force opposing the Prince, but later he had to escape to Skye. Inside this fine building are many exhibits including one very old item, a ten lever spring lock of Dutch make. It originally belonged to George Hutcheson (1560–1639), one of the brothers who founded Hutchesons' Hospital and School.

Crossing West Nile Street it is impossible not to think of the days before mechanical transport when huge Clydesdale horses were used to draw heavy loads up the steep incline of West Nile Street, struggling on their way to Buchanan Street Railway Station and Port Dundas to dispatch their loads.

It might also be remembered that in the days of the horse every street in Glasgow had its colony of birds, including pigeons and sparrows, who fed well on the grain that escaped from the nose bags of the horses when they were feeding in the streets.

We are now coming into the part of Glasgow that was developed when the city was extended westwards from High Street. The large country estate of Blythswood was acquired in the early nineteenth century from Campbell of Blythswood. It lay to the west of Buchanan Street and the houses and business premises standing there today were built around that time. West Campbell Street, Blythswood Street and Blythswood Square perpetuate the name of the proprietor and his estate.

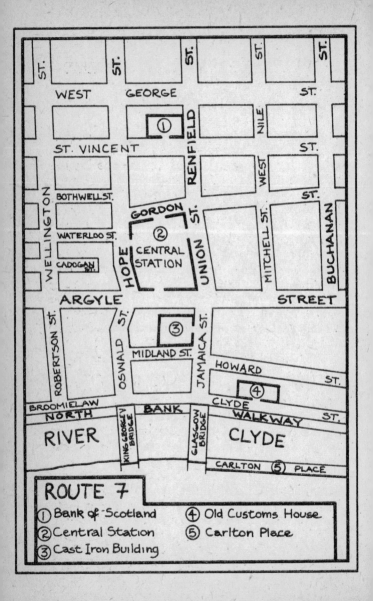

ROUTE 7

① Bank of Scotland
② Central Station
③ Cast Iron Building
④ Old Customs House
⑤ Carlton Place

Route 7

RENFIELD STREET – UNION STREET – JAMAICA STREET – GLASGOW BRIDGE – CARLTON PLACE

Coming to Renfield Street, so named by Campbell of Blythswood after his estate near Renfrew, we turn left and travel down it. On our right is the massive edifice of the Bank of Scotland at 110 St Vincent Street. In the entrance hall is a specie chest dating from 1750 to 1830 which was in use by the Shipbank. At one time the apprentice slept on it at night armed with a blunderbuss to protect the treasure and provided with a bugle to sound the alarm.

Next we come to Gordon Street built on ground belonging to Gordon of Aikenhead and opened in 1802. Also in Gordon Street is the entrance to the Central Station which was once the terminal station for the old Caledonian Railway and now serves all stations in Scotland south of the River Clyde.

Central Station at one time had the largest signal box in the world. This was necessary in order to cope with the vast number of railway lines terminating at the station.

On the wall near the main entrance is an impressive bronze war memorial to approximately 700 men of the old Caledonian Railway who gave their lives in the 1914–18 war.

Central station was built on the site of Grahamston village. A controversy broke out in the daily newspapers a few years ago when it was suggested that the houses and shops of the old village still stood beneath the Railway Station and that a good deal of silverware had been left behind in the shops when the railway company took over the site to build the Central

Station. A good many people were interested in investigating the truth of this fact, particularly scrap dealers, but evidently the old village, if it still did exist, was too difficult to locate beneath the platforms of the station, and there the matter rests, still a mystery to this day.

However, the main street of this village was Alston Street, and it was here in the spring of 1764 that the Playhouse, the first permanent theatre in Glasgow, had its beginning. On two occasions, though, it was partly destroyed by fire and finally ended up as a granary. Shakespeare's statue, which was a feature of the building, now stands in the grounds of a house in Carmunnock. If one looks up Alston Street in one of the old street directories in the Mitchell Library, one will see many of the old shops listed.

We cross Argyle Street, named after Archibald, Duke of Argyle, who in 1761 met his death in England. While en route to the ancestral ducal burial ground at Kilmun, Argyllshire, the body of the Duke lay in state at the Highland Society House in this street.

We now come to Jamaica Street whose name reminds us that Glasgow was once a centre of the rum and sugar trade. At No. 36 is a building erected in 1856. This is the only building in Glasgow with a cast-iron frame.

Crossing over Jamaica Street Bridge or Glasgow Bridge, which spans the River Clyde, we are reminded that the Clyde, famous in song and story, was a great nursery for many famous ships such as *Queen Elizabeth I* and *II*, hence the saying 'Clyde built', signifying the epitome of superb craftsmanship.

This is the third consecutive bridge built to span the river at this point. The first was built in 1768, the second in 1836 and the present one in 1899. A bronze plaque at the centre of the balustrade of the bridge gives a brief history.

To our left is the old Customs House at 298 Clyde Street. It has now been closed and the offices have been moved to Portcullis House, 21 India Street. The wooden board with a list of former excise men that hung in the Collector's Room of the old building is now in the new building as well. Among the names listed is that of Alexander Findlater whose post at that time was deputy to the collector of customs at Port Glasgow. Burns wrote a poem about Findlater entitled 'The Deil's Awa' wi' the Excise Man'. Findlater was buried in North Street Cemetery adjacent to Anderston Old Church, Heddle Place. The Kingston Bridge now sweeps over this site. The church was demolished and the remains from the cemetery removed in 1966 to be reinterred in the Linn Cemetery. However, the Findlater family gravestone can now be seen in its new position in the Linn Cemetery.

Information obtained from H.M. Customs and Excise Library Museum and Records in London, states that Robert Burns was highly efficient in his profession of exciseman and of unblemished character, and he had been selected for promotion to supervisor. Unfortunately, however, he died on 21st July, 1796, shortly before the post fell vacant. His widow Jean Armour drew an excise pension for 37 years, latterly amounting to £12 per year.

In the year 1812 the first steamship ever to be placed in the British Register was registered at the Customs House, Port Glasgow. It was the *Comet* owned by Henry Bell, of Helensburgh, and was built in Port Glasgow. Bell has a monument erected to his memory in Helensburgh which reads:–

Erected in 1872
To the memory of
Henry Bell.

The first in Great Britain who
was successful in practically
applying steam power for the
purpose of navigation.
Born in the county of Linlithgow
in 1766, died in Helensburgh in
1830.

There was also the *Politician,* a boat that featured
in the entertaining film *Whisky Galore.* The records
of the *Politician* are kept in the Customs House
Archives.

The old Customs House, St Andrew's Roman
Catholic Cathedral and Iona Community House,
Clyde Street, are all built on the old Ropework Green
which was owned by James Oswald, whose statue is
standing in George Square. The old Customs House
is on the east bank of the St Enoch's or Glasgow Burn,
which used to be the western boundary of Ropework
Green.

Prior to becoming a walkway, the Customs House
Quay was used by little steam puffers for collecting
granite chips for construction work.

On the south side of Jamaica Bridge is the salmon-
pink and grey coloured terrace of Carlton Place. This
is the first terrace in Glasgow to receive conservation
treatment from grants provided by the Corporation.
The pleasing work was done in 1961 and repeated in
1968.

The terrace was originally built by James Laurie
who gave his name to the district of Laurieston and
had his residence at 51–52 Carlton Place. The interior
plaster work is of exceptionally fine quality. The
building now houses the City of Glasgow Health &
Welfare Department.

At 81 Carlton Place is the Trade Union Centre
which was opened by James Jack, General Secretary

of the Trades Union Congress in 1966. A further extension was opened in 1968 by the Rt. Hon. Lord Provost of Glasgow, John Johnstone.

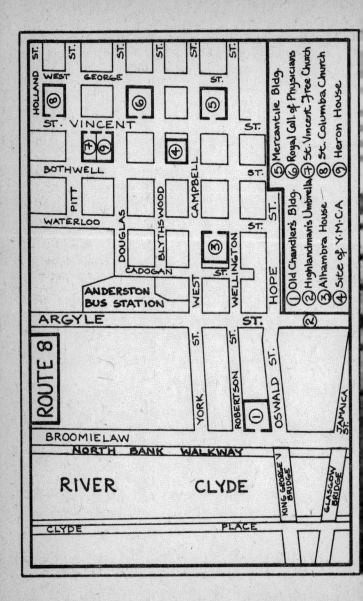

ROUTE 8

1. Old Chandler's Bldg.
2. Highlandman's Umbrella
3. Alhambra House
4. Site of Y.M.C.A.
5. Mercantile Bldg.
6. Royal Coll. of Physicians
7. St. Vincent Free Church
8. St. Columba Church
9. Heron House

ANDERSTON BUS STATION

RIVER   CLYDE

NORTH BANK WALKWAY

BROOMIELAW

CLYDE   PLACE

KING GEORGE V BRIDGE
GLASGOW BRIDGE
JAMAICA ST.

Route 8

KING GEORGE V BRIDGE – OSWALD STREET – HOPE STREET – ST VINCENT STREET

At Clyde Place we turn right to cross King George V Bridge which spans the River Clyde. This is the only bridge on the Clyde with a pedestrian subway. On the eastern balustrade of the bridge is a bronze plaque which states that the memorial stone was laid by His Majesty King George V on 19th July 1927.

On our left is Clyde Place Quay indicated by a clock tower. Directly across the river is the Broomielaw.

It was from these two places that the Clyde pleasure steamers left to take passengers for a day's sail 'doon the watter' to the Clyde holiday resorts or even to embark for the annual holidays. This service no longer exists. A Strathclyde Police Launch, *Semper Vigilo II,* (meaning 'always vigilant' and named after the Glasgow Police motto) is harboured at the Clyde Place Quay and patrols a vast area of waterway covering 7,000 square miles.

On our way north over the King George V Bridge, to our left we observe a ship's chandler's building standing at 72 Broomielaw. On the facade are cut a sailing vessel and the date 1840, and a sign in large letters indicates that it once belonged to Robert Moore and Neill, Ltd., merchants and suppliers of ship's stores. This building has been converted into luxury flats. We continue along Oswald Street, opened in 1817 and named after James Oswald of Shieldhall. Oswald Street is on the western boundary of his property.

Now we cross Argyle Street and enter Hope Street. On the right there is a wide railway bridge crossing in

41

Argyle Street known as the 'Highlanders' Umbrella'. It was here that Highlanders congregated to meet their friends and talk about old times. Of course they never got wet in inclement weather due to the shelter afforded by the overhead railway bridge, hence the name, 'The Highlanders' Umbrella'.

Now we proceed up Hope Street, originally called Copenhagen Street and later renamed in honour of John Hope, 4th Earl of Hopetown who distinguished himself in the Peninsular war. An indication that Glasgow was a seafaring city is clearly seen at No. 45 where a sailing vessel is cut on the stonework above the door of the building known as Atlantic Chambers. We pass, at No. 65–67, the old premises of the newspaper, the *Daily Record*. The building was designed by Robert Thomson and built in 1899. Looking up Waterloo Street from Hope Street we catch a glimpse of the new office block Alhambra House that is built on the site of the Alhambra Theatre, demolished in 1971.

The seven-storied Alhambra House required 250 pylons to be driven to a depth of 40 feet in order to support the building in the sandy soil. Prior to the erection of the Alhambra Theatre the old Wellington Church stood here before its removal to University Avenue, and across the road at the corner of Waterloo Street and Wellington Street stood the old S.M.T. Bus Station, now the site of a new £500,000 office block, Hamilton House, built in 1972 by James Laidlaw the builder.

At the corner of Gordon Street is the entrance to the Central Station Railway Hotel that fronts on to Hope Street, where can be seen above the entrance a lion rampant and on the terrazo tiled floor of the reception hall another lion rampant. The lion being the symbol of the Caledonian Railway, it is easy to see that this was once a Caledonian Railway Hotel. In

Hope Street there stands a large sandstone building between Waterloo Street and Bothwell Street. This fine edifice is now a large office block.

Looking up Bothwell Street, which was named after Bothwell Castle, we see the Y.M.C.A. Buildings described as having the most fantastic architecture in Glasgow. Statues of John Knox and William Tyndal, religious reformers, adorn one facade. All in all, there are three buildings: the Y.M.C.A. Residential Hotel, the Christian Institute and the Bible Training Institute. They were opened in 1879 by Lord Shaftesbury who helped to found the ragged schools.

The buildings will be demolished except for the Bible Training Institute which belongs to the Glasgow Evangelistic Association.

Before turning left into St Vincent Street, we pass Renfield Lane. In this lane is a Charles Rennie Mackintosh building which is very difficult to view owing to the narrowness of the lane.

Around this area in our journey, we can enjoy a wealth of architectural beauty, especially if we take the time to scan the handsome edifices from top to bottom.

Continuing along St Vincent Street, we cross Wellington Street, which crosses Waterloo Street. Both Streets are named in honour of Wellington. Nearby at 131 Wellington Street, stands the Glasgow Ophthalmic Institution founded in 1868 by Dr J. R. Wolfe, an eminent oculist. Dr Wolfe, who was born in Breslau, Germany and died in Glasgow, led a colourful life and was for a while in Sicily with Garibaldi who in 1862 united Italy.

A few yards further on can be seen the statue of a lovely woman. It adorns the edifice at 190 St Vincent Street and is the statue of Recte, Goddess of Justice.

At 200 St Vincent Street there is the North Mercantile Building, erected in 1927. It stands on the site

of the old MacLean's Hotel where Disraeli stayed in
1873 while visiting Glasgow. The two figures above
the door, one female and the other male, symbolise
Prudence and Strength respectively. An interesting
point here is that the sculptor, Archibald Dawson,
was not fully paid for his work and he retaliated by
cutting I.O.U. on the sail of the galleon which adorns
the capital of the column on the right hand side. The
building was designed by Sir John J. Burnet,
(1857–1938) and is one of his masterpieces.

At 242 St Vincent Street stands the Royal College
of Physicians & Surgeons of Glasgow, founded in
1599 by Dr Peter Lowe, a doctor of distinction who
revolutionized the practice of surgery in this country.
He published a book entitled *The Whole Course of
Chirurgie*, printed in London in 1597. It was the first
systematic treatise on the subject produced in this
country and there are only three copies of this edition
in the world. Dr Lowe was buried in the Cathedral
Churchyard in 1612. His tomb can be readily seen
against the wall near the main entrance to the
churchyard. A pair of gloves belonging to Dr Lowe
are on show in the College as well as items associated with Lord Lister of the Royal Infirmary.

As we proceed up St Vincent Street we soon see the
tower of what is now St Vincent Free Church at the
corner of Pitt Street. This is Greek Thomson's
architectural masterpiece. It was built in 1859 and is
one of the finest churches in Europe.

In the Glasgow Necropolis is a massive stone
crowned with the bust of a former minister of this
church. It is near the tomb of William Motherwell, the
poet.

Diagonally across St Vincent Street is the beautiful
red sandstone edifice of the St Columba Church of
Scotland at 298–300. The 200 foot spire is
ornamented by a life-size statue of St Columba. The

church was completed in 1904, and cost £33,000 to build. The previous church was in Hope Street, but was bought in 1900 by the Caledonian Railway Company to make way for the building of the Central Station. The first St Columba Church was built in 1770 where the Royal Bank of Scotland now stands at 110 Queen Street.

A brass plate has been erected inside the present church by members of the clan Mackinnon in remembrance of 232 Mackinnons who fell in the 1914–18 war.

Before turning right into Douglas Street, we notice at 250 St Vincent Street, above the main entrance, the McLean Coat of Arms cut in the stone. This place was once the McLean Hotel (not to be confused with MacLean's Hotel which used to be at 200 St Vincent Street) and then the McGregor's Hotel and was later renamed the Windsor Hotel. It then became the headquarters of the Scotland West Telephone Area before they moved to nearby Heron House. Dr Wolfe, the notable oculist, resided for a while at the Windsor Hotel, and it has also been said that Queen Victoria stayed in this hotel for a brief period during one of her visits to Glasgow.

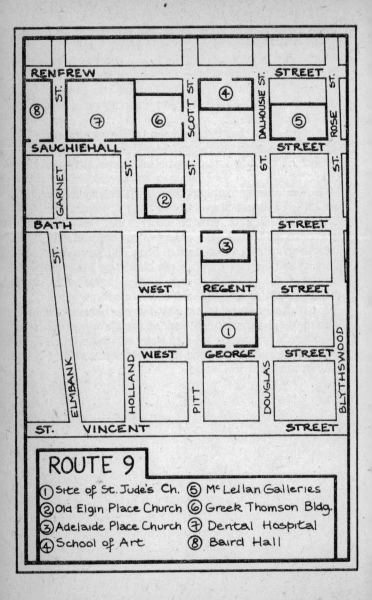

ROUTE 9

① Site of St. Jude's Ch. ⑤ McLellan Galleries
② Old Elgin Place Church ⑥ Greek Thomson Bldg.
③ Adelaide Place Church ⑦ Dental Hospital
④ School of Art ⑧ Baird Hall

Route 9

DOUGLAS STREET – SAUCHIEHALL STREET

Continuing our journey up Douglas Street, we notice to our left a church building at 278/282 West George Street now being let as office space. This was built as an Episcopal church in 1839, and in 1896 it was taken over by St Jude's Free Presbyterian Church which held its last service in Gaelic and English here on 1st January, 1975 before moving to a new building at 133/137 Woodlands Road.

We now skirt Blythswood Square. Madeleine Smith charged in 1857 with poisoning her lover, lived at No. 7.

We then cross Bath Street, so named because William Harley started public baths and large dairy premises here and published a volume on the Harleyan System.

The premises of the 'Queen's Nurses' at 218 Bath Street, opened in 1890, is really a memorial to Mary Higginsbotham, who was the first district nurse in Scotland and perhaps in Britain. She founded the District Nurses Association in 1875, and provided a most helpful service to the city. Later it became affiliated with the Queen Victoria Jubilee Institute for Nurses, and in 1891 the nurses became known as Queen's Nurses. The premises are now a home for single homeless women. The home is operated by the Glasgow Housing Management Department.

Across from here is the Elgin Place Congregational Church, opened in 1856 and closed since 1962. The first minister was the Rev. Alexander Raleigh who was born near Castle Douglas in 1817. The church was referred to as the Wee Cathedral. Alexander

Raleigh belonged to a religious sect called the Cameronians and consisting of the followers of Richard Cameron, who also gave his name to the Cameronian Regiments. The church was the largest Congregational Church in Scotland and held 1200 people. The first church was opened in 1803 and stood on the site of the *Glasgow Herald* offices in Albion Street.

Close by is the Adelaide Place Baptist Church. It is now the only Baptist church in the heart of the city.

Still travelling up Douglas Street, we see on our right, on the wall beside Sauchiehall Lane, the statue of a seated man reading a book to a boy. Below the statue is a bronze tablet with the following words inscribed on it:

City of Glasgow
Friendly Society
Founded by
John Stewart
1862.

The Glasgow Friendly Society not only covers Glasgow but the whole of Britain. It is a breakaway from the Royal Liver Society. The statue represents John Stewart, the founder.

Ahead of us, situated high up at 167 Renfrew Street, we see the School of Art designed by Charles Rennie Mackintosh in 1896.

Turning left into Sauchiehall Street we see on our right the McLennan Galleries at 270 Sauchiehall Street with a bust of Queen Victoria above the main door. This was where the Art Galleries were housed before being removed to Kelvingrove Park, their present site. Directly across the road from here was until recently a house once occupied by Dr Pritchard. It was a rather artistic structure embracing a balcony with ironwork railings and the window sills were decorated with railings to match, but it was demolished in 1978.

Journeying along Sauchiehall Street with its many fine shops and warehouses which make it one of the busiest shopping centres in Glasgow, it is hard to believe that it was once a dreary road with scarcely a house, edged with hedges and running through a 'haugh' or meadow lined with 'saughs' or willows. The name Sauchiehall is a corruption of the Scots word 'Sauchiehaugh'.

At the corner of Scott Street is an Egyptian-style building, designed by Greek Thomson. It resembles the Egyptian Halls in Union Street, but is rather spoiled by a coating of paint.

At 378 Sauchiehall Street are the modern premises of the Glasgow Dental Hospital and School. The premises were opened on 3rd December, 1970, by H.R.H. The Duchess of Kent.

The school was originally founded in 1879 in the old Anderson College in George Street, and a hospital was built later.

The first man to obtain the degree of Licentiate of Dental Surgery (L.D.S.) was William Stead Woodburn of Glasgow, in 1879, and this gave him the licence to practice. Prior to this anyone could practice as a dentist whether they had the skill or not.

It will be seen as we travel down Sauchiehall Street than many of the old traditional tenements bordering the street are on the point of being demolished. They were built of sandstone drawn from the local quarries, but in their place will be erected buildings built of concrete and steel, truly an indication of an advance into another age.

Soon we come to the eight-storied edifice at 460 Sauchiehall Street, now the University of Strathclyde, Baird Hall of Residence. It was originally built and opened as the Beresford Hotel for the 1938 Empire

Exhibition which was held in Bellahouston Park. Baird Hall is named after John Logie Baird (1888–1946) the inventor of television in whose honour a bronze bust has been placed in the vestibule of the hall, where there is much of his early equipment on show.

John Logie Baird was born in Helensburgh and he started work for the Clyde Valley Electrical Power Company as a superintendent engineer.

At 474 Sauchiehall Street was the firm of monumental sculptors, John Gray & Company. This firm repaired the Stone of Destiny, when it was broken during its unofficial removal from Westminster Abbey to Scotland in 1950. The firm has recently moved elsewhere.

It is also interesting to know that their founder William W. Gray designed the Heraldic Lions made of alabaster in 1885 for the City Chambers.

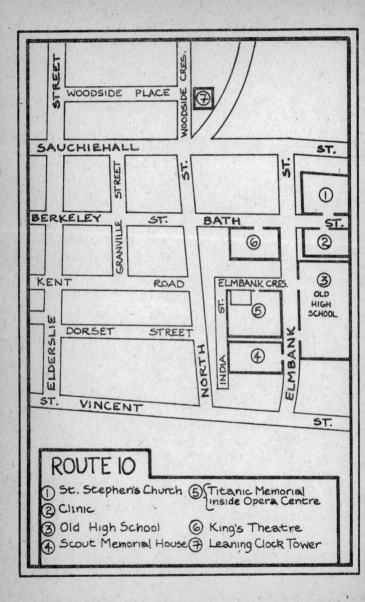

ROUTE 10

① St. Stephen's Church ⑤ Titanic Memorial inside Opera Centre
② Clinic
③ Old High School ⑥ King's Theatre
④ Scout Memorial House ⑦ Leaning Clock Tower

Route 10

ELMBANK STREET – BATH STREET

Before we turn into Elmbank Street we get a glimpse of Sauchiehall Street looking towards Charing Cross. We see the Tiffany Dance Hall that used to be the Locarno, at one time one of Glasgow's popular dance halls.

We walk down Elmbank Street and turn right into Bath Street. We are now in the centre of a very interesting part of Glasgow.

At 260 Bath Street is the Neo-Gothic edifice of the Renfield St Stephen's Church, and also the Renfield Church Centre opened in 1969 and known since 1977 as Renfield Saint Stephen's Church Centre. The Renfield Church which stood on the corner of Sauchiehall Street and Renfield Street was demolished in 1964.

Renfield Church Centre is actually a union of 12 churches which stood in the neighbourhood but were demolished due to the redevelopment of the city.

Inside this cathedral-like church are many war memorials from the 12 original churches. They are a silent testimony to the hundreds who fell in the two world wars.

Opposite here at 279 Bath Street is a building which has been used as the Glasgow Physiotherapy and Rehabilitation Clinic since 1930. Before this it was occupied jointly by the Bath Street United Free Church and the Berkeley Street United Free Church. As a result, there are still war memorials from the two churches inside the building. The Bath Street memorial is dedicated to 23 men killed during the 1914–18 war and the Berkeley Street plaque lists 52 men who fell in the same war. Berkeley Street United Free

Church was later renovated and served as the High-landers' Institute until 1979.

The nearby ten-storied Elmbank Chambers at 289 Bath Street, stands on the site of the City Temple, last used as a place of worship by the Pentecostal Church.

Four statues adorn the facade of the former High School in Elmbank Street and probably symbolise learning. The school had its beginnings in Greyfriars Wynd, now known as Nicholas Street. Later it was in John Street.

We learn from reading the inscriptions on the stones built into the wall of the building that one of them was taken from the lintel of the doorway at the back of the old Grammar School in Greyfriars Wynd which was demolished in 1874 during the time of the City Improvement Trust. The other stones were removed in 1878 from the Grammar School in John Street.

On the walls of the Assembly Hall are the names, often accompanied by pictures or features in bronze, of distinguished men who were former pupils of the school such as Bonar Law (1858–1923), Henry Campbell Bannerman (1836–1908), William Elphinstone (1431–1514), George Buchanan (1506–1582), General Sir John Moore, the hero of Corunna and Lord Clyde. The last two have a statue each to their honour in George Square standing side by side.

Also on show on the wall of the staircase is a facsimile of the 1320 Declaration of Scottish Independence, presented by a Burns Club.

The High School has now been moved elsewhere and the Strathclyde Region are spending £3½ million to convert the building for their use. At present the Region are temporarily occupying Melrose House, Glasgow.

Across the road from the High School at 21 Elmbank Street, is the Scout Memorial House, and a plaque on the wall inside the premises relates a brief history of the house as follows.

This house was acquired, named and
dedicated to the glorious and undying
memory of the Scouts of Glasgow, who
fought and died for King and Country
in the Great War 1914–18.
Say not that the brave die.

There is also a further bronze plaque to the memory of Robert E. Young, County Commissioner from 1907 to 1940, who was the founder of the Scout Movement in Glasgow.

The strength of the Boy Scout Movement in Glasgow is about 13,000, approximately the same as that of the Boys' Brigade in the city.

Next door to the Scout Memorial Hall, at 23 Elmbank Street, is the Tom Allan Centre, founded by Tom Allan, a notable minister of St George's Tron Church.

The old Institute of Engineering and Shipbuilders at 39 Elmbank Crescent, is now the premises of Scottish Opera Limited and Scottish Theatre Ballet, founded in 1962 and now equal to any other opera company in Europe. Strangely enough, it has a link with the Grand Hotel that at one time stood in Charing Cross.

The Grand Hotel was demolished in 1969 in order to make way for the inner ring road or M8. A plaque which was situated inside the main entrance was saved and given to the Scottish Opera. The plaque was to the memory of Eugene D'Albert, composer and pianist, who was born in the Grand Hotel in 1864. It had been erected in 1941 by the Dunedin Society. It is now in the entrance hall of the Scottish Opera.

Here there is also a memorial to the 36 engineers of the *Titanic,* who all died on 15th April, 1912, when the ship was lost in mid-Atlantic. The memorial was erected by the Institution of Engineers and Shipbuilders in Scotland.

Also in the Rankine Hall are some fine stained glass windows depicting sailing vessels, steam locomotives and steamships.

At the corner of Elmbank Street and Bath Street is the King's Theatre, one of Glasgow's few remaining theatres. It was built in 1905 and since then has provided a high standard of entertainment. The King's Theatre mascot is a little stone lion holding a shield which surmounts the entrance. It is often referred to as the Lion of Bath Street.

Continuing our journey along Bath Street, we notice on our left that India Street, once a fashionable residential area which included the old world More's Hotel, has all been demolished and in its place stand multi-storied office blocks: a doubtful exchange for old-fashioned elegance and gracious living.

Soon we cross a road bridge that spans the approach road to the Kingston Bridge. When the approach road was built, all the tenements, including the Headquarters of the St Andrew's Ambulance Association, had to be demolished and the Charing Cross Railway Station shifted, in order to make way for the road. The St Andrew's Ambulance Association now have new Headquarters in Milton Street opened in 1970 by the Queen Mother.

To our right at this point can be seen the wide sweep of Charing Cross, bordered by the handsome Charing Cross Mansions, complete with an ornate clock, ten sculptured figures and the Glasgow Coat of Arms with the motto 'Let Glasgow Flourish'.

Here is the Road Bridge Folly that leads nowhere. It is available for office or entertainment development on a two-storied basis and it is hoped that in the future such a building will surmount the bridge and at the same time span the roadway. Here is also Glasgow's own leaning tower, the fountain that leans at a perceptible angle.

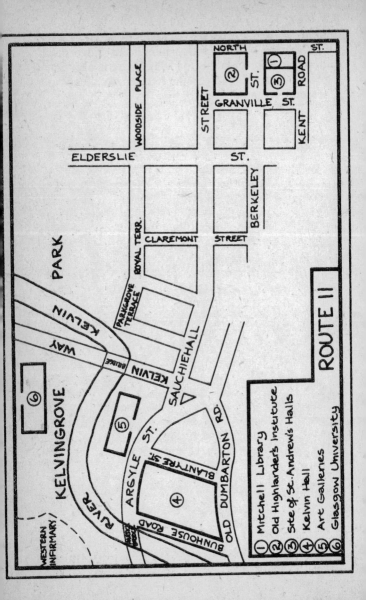

ROUTE II

① Mitchell Library
② Old Highlander's Institute
③ Site of St. Andrew's Halls
④ Kelvin Hall
⑤ Art Galleries
⑥ Glasgow University

Route 11

BERKELEY STREET – ELDERSLIE STREET – SANDYFORD PLACE – SAUCHIEHALL STREET

Shortly we enter Berkeley Street, and to our left is the pleasing edifice of the Mitchell Library, the largest public library in Scotland, containing around a million volumes. The dome of the library is appropriately surmounted by the figure of Minerva, Goddess of Wisdom and patroness of all the arts. In the entrance hall of the library is a marble bust dedicated to the founder of the library, Stephen Mitchell, born 19th September 1789, died 2nd April 1874.

The Highlanders' Institute was once at 34 Berkeley Street and most of the clans associations in the Glasgow area used it for meetings and functions.

Walking down Berkeley Street, we cross Granville Street where St Andrew's Halls once stood. This building unfortunately suffered damage in a fire some years ago and was taken over by the Mitchell Library.

The beautiful facade, including the skilfully cut statues and ornate main entrance in Granville Street, however, survived. High up on the facade are inscribed the names Raphael, Watt, Michael Angelo, Newton, Flaxman, Purcell, Bach, Handel, Mozart and Beethoven, which represent the arts and the sciences.

Still walking along Berkeley Street we admire the terraced houses built over a hundred years ago by the old time craftsmen.

At number 66 Berkeley Street there is no evidence when we look at the quiet exterior that once a murder was committed here, but it was, back in 1865, and the perpetrator has been under discussion ever since, namely Dr Pritchard who was later hanged for his many crimes.

Completing our journey along Elderslie Street, we turn left into Sandyford Place and again we encounter a house at No. 17 Sandyford Place where a murder was committed. Again the quiet exterior belies its past history, because it was here that Jessie McLachlan was accused of murdering her friend. She served a prison sentence for this.

Practically all the terraced houses in Sandyford Place have been converted into business premises. Reminiscent of even further changes in the area is a huge concrete and glass building facing Sandyford Place known as Clifton House which is Scottish Health Service, Building Division Headquarters.

Going along Sauchiehall Street and looking down Claremont Street near Fitzroy Lane we find, cut on a stone built into the gable end of an adjacent building, the following words:-

Glasgow
Botanic Gardens
Instituted
1817.

It is on record that there previously was a similar garden in the old college in High Street, established in 1705 for teaching purposes. In 1842 the gardens in Fitzroy Lane were removed to their present site.

It has been stated that No. 6 Fitzroy Place has the finest door in Glasgow and on close observation it can be seen that it is the premises of the Scottish Painters Society. The door is decorated with an oval of stained glass and the carved head of a cherub. Directly across the road is Royal Crescent, screened by a number of trees. At No. 22 Royal Crescent is yet another house where Dr Pritchard resided at one time.

This area is aptly called the 'Square Mile of Murder' due to the fact that four classic murders were committed here. Three cases have already been mentioned, namely those of Madeleine Smith, Jessie McLachlan and Dr Pritchard. The fourth was Oscar Slater who was accused of murdering Miss Gilchrist of West Princes Street. After serving a term of imprisonment for the murder, he was granted a reprieve.

Around this area there are many small hotels which are conveniently situated in an interesting part of Glasgow. This can be seen when shortly we turn right into Kelvin Way, for at this point we have a splendid panoramic view of the Kelvin Hall, which was built in 1927 and numbers among one of the largest exhibition centres in the British Commonwealth. Close by are the Art Galleries, opened in 1902 and housing most of Glasgow's art collection which is one of the finest in Britain.

Situated nearby on Gilmorehill is the main building of Glasgow University, designed by Sir George Gilbert Scott after the University was moved here from High Street in 1870.

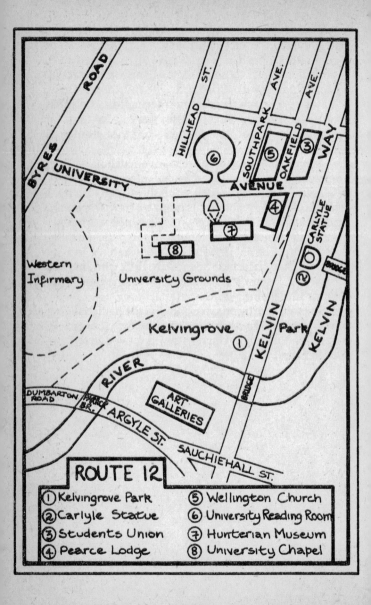

ROUTE 12

① Kelvingrove Park
② Carlyle Statue
③ Students Union
④ Pearce Lodge
⑤ Wellington Church
⑥ University Reading Room
⑦ Hunterian Museum
⑧ University Chapel

Route 12

KELVIN WAY – UNIVERSITY AVENUE–BYRES ROAD

Going up Kelvin Way, we pass several bowling greens and croquet lawns, all within the confines of Kelvingrove Park which was acquired in 1852. This beautiful park is immortalised by the song *Kelvin Grove* written by Dr Thomas Lyle. The first stanza runs thus

Let us haste to Kelvingrove Bonnie Lassie O'
Thro its mazes let us rove Bonnie Lassie O'
Where the rose in all her pride
Paints the hollow dingle side
Where the midnight fairies glide Bonnie Lassie O'

Shortly after entering Kelvin Way we pass over a bridge that spans the River Kelvin. There are four groups of bronze statues on the bridge that represent Commerce and Industry; Peace and War; Navigation and Shipping and Progress and Prosperity. These statues were selected from a competition held before 1914, but were not erected until 1926. They were badly damaged by enemy action during the night of 13th March, 1941, and restored by Benno Schotz R.S.A.

Further along Kelvin Way on the right hand side in Kelvingrove Park is a seated statue of William Thomson, Lord Kelvin, born in Belfast in 1824. He did a great deal to further the general use of electricity. A few yards away is another statue depicting Lord Lister in a meditative mood. He was born in Upton, Essex, but he lived in a house not far distant at No. 17 Woodside Place.

He was a leading surgeon who discovered antiseptics. Not far away is a modern piece of sculpture representing a psalmist by Benno Schotz erected in memory of Dr Tom Honeyman who was Director of Glasgow Art Galleries (1939–1954) and Rector of Glasgow University (1953–1956).

On the left hand side of Kelvin Way, still in Kelvingrove Park, is a rough block of granite surmounted by a chiselled bust of Thomas Carlyle, the Scottish thinker who was born in Ecclefechan, Dumfriesshire in 1795. The memorial faces the Prince of Wales Bridge which spans the River Kelvin and at the other end of the bridge is the sculptured figure of a soldier mounted on a pedestal.

On Kelvin Way, near University Avenue, was planted on 20th April, 1918, the Sufferage Oak to commemorate the granting of votes to women.

At No. 1 University Avenue is the church of the Congregational Union of Scotland. Close to this church at 9–11 University Avenue is a former church now the property of the University and known as Gilmorehill Hall. This hall originally belonged to Anderston Free Church which started in Clyde Street in the then village of Anderston and came to be known as Gilmorehill Church of Scotland after being moved here in 1879.

Across the road from here is the Men's Students Union which is actually a memorial to a Dr McIntyre's wife.

The original Students Union was officially opened in 1890, but it is now used as a bookshop and stands at the main entrance to the University in University Avenue. The present Men's Students Union was opened in 1931.

Across from here in University Avenue is Pearce Lodge which was the original lodge of the old University when it stood in High Street, prior to its removal in 1870. It could be said to be the oldest building in University Avenue as it was rebuilt in 1887 on its present site as a result of the efforts of Sir William Pearce, Govan shipbuilder.

Further along University Avenue, at the corner of Southpark Avenue, is the Wellington Church, built in 1884 and designed by Thomas Lennox Watson. It is similar in design to the Madeleine in Paris and is called Wellington Church because the previous church stood in Wellington Street. It is interesting to note that among the names listed on the war memorials on display inside the church there are very few privates. They are mostly all officers, indicating, that in the past this was a church with a congregation of wealthy people.

The Wellington Church has been united with Woodlands Road Church of Scotland since 1974 and the latter church has been bought and renovated by St Judes Free Presbyterian Church of Scotland which was formerly at 278 West George Street.

Quite near the Wellington Church is the University Reading Room, perhaps the most unusually shaped building in Glasgow, for it is round and dome shaped. In 1949 this building won the Royal Institute of British Architects Award.

In University Avenue, directly across from the reading room, is an ornate wrought-iron gate with the dates 1451–1951 and the motto of the University *Via Veritas Vita* which means, 'the Way, the Truth, and the Life'. On the gate are 28 names of former students who have made their mark in the world. For instance there is John Glaister, the founder of forensic medicine. Glasgow University was once the only place where this discipline could be studied. Glaister himself played a prominent role as a medico-legal examiner in the Oscar Slater trial of 1909.

Directly behind the wrought iron gates is a monument to the memory of William Hunter (1718–83) and John Hunter (1723–93), world-famous doctors.

They were born at Long Calderwood, East Kilbride, where there is now a museum.

William Hunter left a valuable collection of a wide range of items rarely equalled by a private collector to Glasgow University. This collection is now housed in the Hunterian Museum.

Incorporated into the wall inside the main entrance of the University is a stone that has an indirect link with Greyfriars Monastery. On it are the words

Old stone from
near Greyfriars Churchyard
Thomas Reid
Professor of Philosophy.

Thomas Reid was Professor of Moral Philosophy in 1764 in the old University in High Street.

The University chapel was built in 1929 and was dedicated to the seven hundred and fifty-five sons of the University who were killed in the 1914–18 war. Leading to the chapel is the lion and unicorn staircase which was removed from the old University in High Street and rebuilt here in 1872.

Passing University Gardens which were once private residences and are now the property of the University, we come to number 7 which was once the house of Dr Charles Hepburn. It was here that the New Glasgow Society was founded. It is now called Hepburn House and the Hepburn Coat of Arms decorates the door.

In University Avenue, near the Botany Building, is a small section of decorative grassland, where can be seen a petrified tree stump. There is nothing to indicate where this important fossil came from and one is left to guess at its origin.

Soon we come to Byres Road which was named after a small village or 'clachan' called Byres of Partick. It was proposed at one time to rename it Victoria

Road. Strangely enough, the present Victoria Road in Crosshill is very similar to Byres Road. They were both built in the Victorian era and are equally good shopping centres.

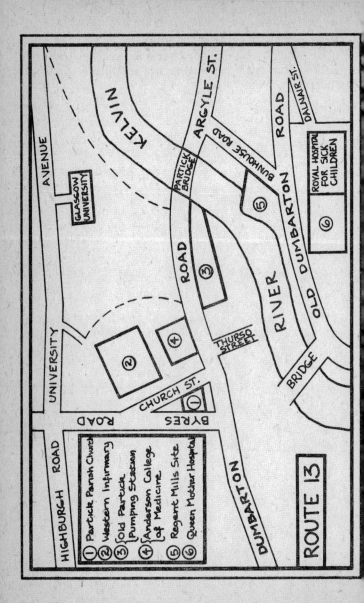

ROUTE 13

HIGHBURGH ROAD

UNIVERSITY

AVENUE

KELVIN

ARGYLE ST.

DALNAIR ST.

GLASGOW
UNIVERSITY

ROAD

PARTICK
BRIDGE

BUNHOUSE ROAD

DUMBARTON

ROAD

ROAD

③

⑤

RIVER

OLD DUMBARTON

ROYAL HOSPITAL
FOR SICK
CHILDREN

⑥

②

④

THURSO
STREET

BRIDGE

BYRES   ROAD

CHURCH ST.

①

DUMBARTON

① Partick Parish Church
② Western Infirmary
③ Old Partick
    Pumping Station
④ Anderson College
    of Medicine
⑤ Regent Mills Site
⑥ Queen Mother Hospital

68

Route 13

CHURCH STREET – DUMBARTON ROAD – PARTICK BRIDGE

We turn left at Byres Road, walk a bit and then turn left into Church Street so called after the old Partick Parish Church which still stands at No. 11. It was founded in 1834, rebuilt in 1879 and extended in 1895.

Also in the church is a war memorial which was placed here after its removal from the neighbouring Church Street Public School, which has now been taken over by the Glasgow Social Works Department.

It is interesting to note that although the school is in the district of Partick, cut on the facade are the words

Church Street Public School
Govan Parish School Board,

indicating that Partick was once in the Parish of Govan.

At the front entrance to the church is a memorial to John Smith, D.D., whose wife unveiled the war memorial. It is interesting to note that the Rev. Smith was born in Tollcross in 1854, and died in Glasgow in 1927. Tollcross was a separate district, and not a part of Glasgow, but was annexed to the city in 1912.

There are many beautiful stained glass windows in this church, including one dedicated to Queen Victoria.

The buildings on the triangle of ground between Church Street and Byres Road are earmarked for demolition in order to extend the Western Infirmary. It is hoped to renovate the buildings fronting Dumbarton Road and Byres Road.

All along the left side of Church Street lies the Western Infirmary which was completed in 1874. Around this time, due to its proximity to the University, it was also used for instructing medical students who till then were trained at the Royal Infirmary. However, later the Royal Infirmary was again used for this purpose.

The Western Infirmary has been extended greatly since its inception. At 38 Church Street is the Tennent Memorial Building ornamented with two stone figures above the main entrance.

There is also the Alexander Elder Memorial Building built in 1923 as a nurses' home. Elder also provided the chapel named after him and situated on the first floor of the G Wing.

An unusual and interesting bronze plaque adorns the wall of a corridor near A Block. On it are the words

In memory of Charles
Lutwidge Dodgson, Lewis Carroll
in grateful recognition of his
services to children.
Erected by his admirers
in Glasgow and West Coast
of Scotland.

A common feature of many of Glasgow's infirmaries is the sculptured figure of a puma. The Western Infirmary has two on display; one cut on the gable end of a wing of A Block, and surmounting the gable end of another wing of the same block is the complete stone figure of a puma. The reason for the puma being used as a symbol by the infirmaries is that this animal is considered the nurse of the jungle.

At the bottom of Church Street, before turning left at Dumbarton Road we notice on our right a public house named Reids of Pertyck. This is the old name of

Partick. It is said that at one time a thatched cottage stood on this site that was used as an alehouse.

A little further on, at 33 Dumbarton Road, there is a fine red sandstone building by the Kelvin River. A plaque outside reads

Glasgow Main Drainage
Partick Pumping Station
Inaugurated on 30th May, 1904.

This pumping station was in use by the Burgh of Partick before it was annexed to Glasgow in 1912.

Thanks to the River Purification Act of 1971, small fish can once again be seen swimming in the river, and we can always hope that one day the famous salmon will return as well.

Facing the pumping station at 56 Dumbarton Road is the Anderson College of Medicine. This was the last building to be designed by James Sellars and it was finished by John Keppie, the noted architect.

Also facing Dumbarton Road are the embossed figures of ten serious-looking men, one of whom is in the act of feeling the pulse of a patient, which seems to symbolise the medical profession. The sculptor of this work was Pittendrigh Macgillivray.

On display inside the building is a portion of the cross section of a tree. A small brass plate attached gives its interesting history and reads as follows:–

This is a section of a branch
from the Punda Tree, Livingstonia,
Northern Rhodesia, under or near
which the heart of David Livingstone
was buried by his servants and followers.
Livingstone received his medical
education at this College.

It is said that the basement of this college is haunted, a rumour perhaps caused by the fact that in the early days the basement was used for dissecting bodies.

The building now forms part of Glasgow University and houses the dermatology and microbiology departments.

We now cross Partick Bridge which spans the River Kelvin. There are a total of four plaques, one at each corner of the bridge, giving a brief history of its construction.

Near the bridge on the east side of the River Kelvin, in Bunhouse Road, used to be the immense derelict buildings of the Regent Flour Mills. The words 'Regent Mills' signify a lot in Glasgow history for it was during the Battle of Langside in 1568 that Regent Moray, who commanded the army opposing his half-sister Mary Queen of Scots was supplied with bread for his troops by the Incorporation of Bakers founded in 1556. In return for their services the Regent presented them with the mills at Partick and a portion of land around it. Nearby Regent Moray Street perpetuates his name.

The Regent Flour Mills were demolished in 1978 so that the riverside could be landscaped as part of the Kelvin Walkway. The adjacent Bishop's Mill is a listed building and it is intended that it will be turned into an art workshop centre, if finances are available.

Across the murky waters of the River Kelvin from where the Regent Mills used to stand we see Spillers Mills. Inside, placed on the wall in a glass case, are a few items of historic interest that were contained inside what is known as the Scotstoun Bottle. A letter attached gives a brief history. An extract from it runs 'This bottle was inserted in the wall on 28th April, 1899, by John White, Provost of Partick, proprietor of Scotstoun Grain Mill'.

The tower was demolished in June, 1973, in preparation for the erection of a new single storey flour warehouse on the same site.

Nearby on Yorkhill is the Royal Hospital for Sick Children. Adjacent to this hospital is the Queen Mother Hospital which was opened by the Queen Mother in 1964. The Queen Mother was formerly the Duchess of York. As well as giving her name to the hospital, she has also given her emblem, the White Rose of York, to be used as part of the present emblem of the hospital badge and, of course, the name Yorkhill is a further connection with the emblem. A large picture of the Queen hangs proudly on the entrance wall of the hospital.

The emblem of the Sick Children's Hospital is, appropriately enough, a mother and child.

The view from the well-kept grounds of the hospital is excellent and the *Waverley* Paddle Steamer can be readily seen sailing up and down the River Clyde. Its embarkation point is at Anderston Quay. It is the last seagoing paddle steamer in the world.

Next to the hospital in Yorkhill Parade is the Headquarters of the 71st Engineers Regiment.

Yorkhill was in the eighteenth century part of Overnewton Estate. A Glasgow merchant, Robert Fulton Alexander, acquired the lands at this period and in 1805 built Yorkhill House. Later the estate became the property of John Graham Gilbert the famous painter. Gilbert Street in Yorkhill carries the family name. He died in Yorkhill House in 1866. The house was demolished in 1911 and streets were constructed through the land.

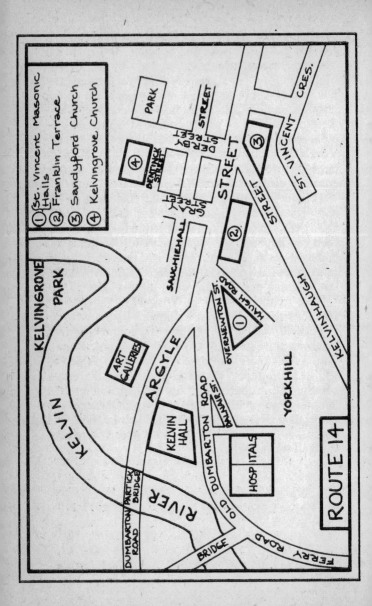

ROUTE 14

Route 14

ARGYLE STREET

Walking down Argyle Street we notice on our left to the west of the Art Galleries a fine memorial depicting three members of the Cameronians (Scottish Rifles) in action. A plaque indicates that the 6th and 7th Batallions of the Cameronians were disbanded on 31st March, 1967, and the First Regular Batallion on 4th May, 1968, thus ending the regiment's long military association with Glasgow. This plaque was unveiled by the Rt. Hon. John Johnstone, Lord Provost of Glasgow. The colours of the Cameronians hang in the nave of Glasgow Cathedral.

Many of the streets round about are named after well-known personalities of Glasgow's past. For instance, nearby is Lumsden Street that took its name from Sir James Lumsden, who was Lord Provost of the City from 1866–69. There is a statue erected in 1862 in Cathedral Square to the memory of his father, James Lumsden, who was also Lord Provost of the City from 1843–46.

Blackie Street takes its name from John Blackie who was Lord Provost of Glasgow in 1862, and Blantyre Street keeps alive the memory of Baron Blantyre (1818–1900) who was twelfth Baron of Erskine House and Lennoxlove.

Passing the junction of Overnewton Street and Haugh Road we see the fine red sandstone building of the St Vincent Masonic Halls, designed by Sinclair and Ballantyne and built at the amazingly small cost of £5,500.

The Masonic Halls is a listed Grade C building. The halls, at present vacant, will be preserved and the nearby houses numbering 15–21 and 33–41 Blackie

Street will also be renovated under the Yorkhill Local Area Plan.

Further along Argyle Street we come to Kelvinhaugh Street, built on the 'haugh' or hollow leading to the village of Kelvinhaugh. At No. 13 Kelvinhaugh Street there is Sandyford-Henderson Memorial Church. This church was originally built as Sandyford Church at a cost of £9,000 and opened for worship in 1855. George Mathieson, D.D., L.L.D., the blind minister of Innellan Church from 1868–1886, who composed the hymn 'O Love That Wilt Not Let Me Go', was assistant minister here in 1867. Then the union with Henderson Memorial Church took place in 1938, and following this, another distinguished assistant minister, J. Pitt Watson, who was Moderator of the General Assembly in 1953 and the first Moderator to take part in a Coronation at Westminster Abbey, served here.

The building that had once housed Henderson Memorial Church in Lumsden Street was intact until some years ago when parts of it burned down. The hall and the offices, however, were saved and are now being used by an engineering firm.

Before passing Derby Street we should note the College and Kelvingrove United Free Church which was rebuilt after being burnt down in 1925. The fire is thought to have started from sparks flying from the Kelvin Hall which had caught fire.

William Smith (1854–1914) who founded the world-famous Boys Brigade in 1883 was a member and church elder of the College and Kelvingrove United Free Church.

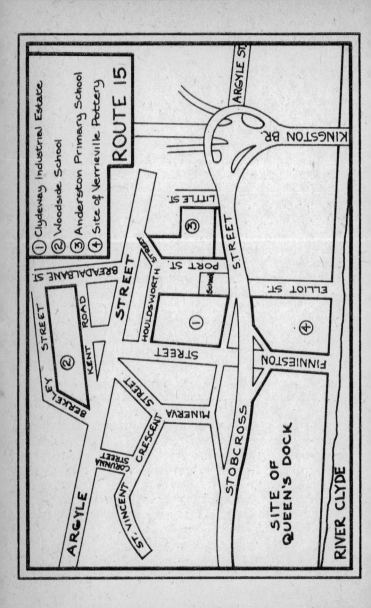

ROUTE 15

① Clydeway Industrial Estate
② Woodside School
③ Anderston Primary School
④ Site of Verrieville Pottery

Route 15

CORUNNA STREET –
ST VINCENT CRESCENT –
MINERVA STREET –
STOBCROSS STREET

We now arrive at Corunna Street named in honour of Sir John Moore's victory over Napoleon in 1809. There is also a statue of Moore in George Square and a plaque marking the place of his birth in Trongate. We walk down Corunna Street and turn left at St Vincent Crescent, the longest crescent in Glasgow, named in honour of a victory over the Spaniards by Sir John Jervis in 1797 off Cape St Vincent, Portugal.

Turning right into Minerva Street, we find part of it has been demolished for industrial purposes.

Clearly visible as we walk along is the huge crane situated at Stobcross Quay, Berth No. 52, and labelled crane No. 5. At one time it was the largest in Europe. It was built in 1932, is 175 feet high and could lift 175 tons, (now reduced to 160 tons), and it was capable of loading steam locomotives for shipment from the now defunct North British Locomotive Works, Springburn.

The vast network of iron at the top of the crane is the popular roost of many birds and it has been reported that two sparrow hawks mate here every spring and consequently during this period scare the other birds away. Beside the huge crane is a helicopter pad which is used for general purposes.

To our right can be seen the Queen's Dock. The dock basin was filled in with the debris from St Enochs Hotel and Station, demolished in 1978, and also the excavations from the new Glasgow Underground System. All is now quiet and tranquil and it seems hard to believe that great ships once anchored here amidst the hustle and the bustle when the Clyde was a great shipping port.

Turning into Stobcross Street, on our left we see the old Finnieston Street Railway Station. There is the emblem of the old Caledonian Railway, the Lion Rampant, cut on a stone above the main entrance.

Crossing over Finnieston Street, we pass the Clydeway Industrial Estate, which is built on the site of Grace Street and is perhaps the biggest of its kind in Scotland.

At the corner of Breadalbane Street and St Vincent Street, was the Grove Boxing Stadium run by Johnnie McMillan, Scottish Featherweight champion, where many notable boxers of the area did their training – among them Peter Keenan, British Empire and European Flyweight Champion, and also British Empire and European Bantamweight Champion; Jackie Paterson, World Flyweight Champion and Peter Reilly, Light Heavyweight Champion.

Next to old Finnieston Street School in Stobcross Street is the New Anderston Primary School which replaced the primary schools that were once in use in this area. The school was opened by Bailie McCann around 1972, and in 1973 Princess Margaret visited the school and planted a tree in the grounds in memory of her visit.

South of Stobcross Street and between Finnieston Street and Elliot Street was once the renowned Verreville Pottery, one of the most interesting factories in our city. Some of their greatly-prized products made here can be seen at the People's Palace Museum, Glasgow Green.

Finnieston village in the early nineteenth century consisted of thatched cottages and the merchants of Glasgow went there to spend their summer holidays.

It will be noticed that Hydepark Street and Lancefield Street are still paved with cobble stones and it might be rememberd that the old Hydepark Locomotive Works were founded in 1836 in Hydepark Street and later in 1862 removed to Springburn. They are now defunct.

There is a lot of magic in the street names around this quarter of Anderston, names from far flung places such as Washington, Whitehall, Cheapside and Piccadilly. It has even been vaguely hinted that the area around the Anderston Electrical Works in Elliot Street at one time belonged to a German Count.

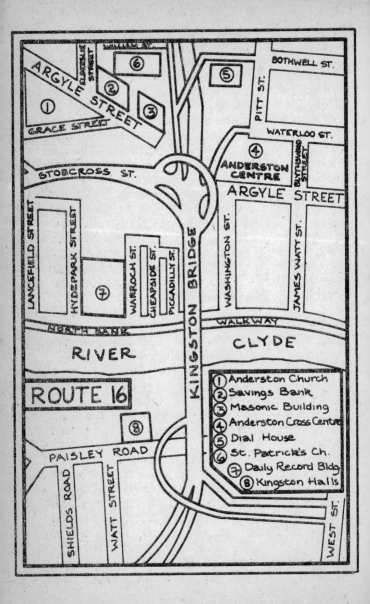

ARGYLE STREET

WILLIAM STREET

ELDERSLIE STREET

BOTHWELL ST.

⑥

②

⑤

PITT ST.

①

③

GRACE STREET

WATERLOO ST.

STOBCROSS ST.

④ ANDERSTON CENTRE

BLYTHSWOOD STREET

ARGYLE STREET

LANCEFIELD STREET

HYDEPARK STREET

WARROCH ST.

CHEAPSIDE ST.

PICCADILLY ST.

WASHINGTON ST.

JAMES WATT ST.

KINGSTON BRIDGE

⑦

HEATH BANK

WALKWAY

RIVER

CLYDE

ROUTE 16

① Anderston Church
② Savings Bank
③ Masonic Building
④ Anderston Cross Centre
⑤ Dial House
⑥ St. Patrick's Ch.
⑦ Daily Record Bldg
⑧ Kingston Halls

⑧

PAISLEY ROAD

SHIELDS ROAD

WATT STREET

WEST ST.

Route 16

KINGSTON BRIDGE

If you intend travelling by motor car, let us continue
our journey and ascend on to the Kingston Bridge.
What a breathtaking view you get of the surrounding
area! The old and the new are delightfully blended
together, forming a kaleidoscope of magnificent
scenery, and what an interesting story these old and
new buildings can tell!

First, on our left we see the pointed green copper
roof of Anderston Parish Church. A few yards from
this church at 1752 Argyle Street is what used to be
the Cranstonhill Branch of the Savings Bank of Glasgow. The unusually designed doorway resembles an
altar in a church. This bank was closed in 1975. The
adjacent computer centre, however, is still open.

Further on, at 650 Argyle Street, standing like a
lone sentinel amid much desolation is the old Masonic
Building (built in 1869) with a number of recognised
masonic signs cut on its facade. In the lower part of
the building is the Shandon Bells Public House where
there are on display a number of pictures of old
Anderston. Close by once stood the old Weavers'
Building, now demolished. The items recovered from
the foundation stone are on show at the People's
Palace.

Beside the Weavers' Building was Crieff Court,
where there was a boxing club. It will be rememberd
that George Judge, boxer, who lived in Anthony
Street, and Ambrose Blackburn, amateur boxer, did
their training in this gone-but-not-forgotten boxing
club. Two amateur teams were also once recruited
from the streets of this now largely derelict, vandal-
ised and ruined area. They were the Anderston Ben-
burb and Finnieston Hearts and both teams wore

maroon jerseys and practised on a football pitch in Whitehall Street.

Oddly enough, it was Crieff Court, Anderston, that King Edward VIII visited in 1936 in order to see a typical city slum. At one house he visited, a little boy asked him if he was really the King. The King doffed his hat good naturedly and told him he was.

Lying partly under the pillars of Kingston Bridge can be seen the old Stobcross Railway Station. The platforms, which generations of feet trod, are forlorn and unattended but still reasonably intact. Close by, under the vast pillars was the site of Anderston Parish Heddle Place Church complete with graveyard. The remains were removed to Linn Cemetery prior to the building of the Kingston Road Bridge, and the church is now incorporated into the New Anderston Parish Church.

The second minister of Heddle Place Church was the Rev. James Steuart, a son of Bonnie Prince Charlie. It was the Queen Mother who opened the Kingston Bridge in 1970.

Looking east along Argyle Street, we observe the new Anderston Cross Centre with its three tall buildings that were named after vessels that sailed from Anderston Quay, namely Davaar, Dalriada and Columba. There are also four office blocks named Hannah House, May House, Angus House and Rankin House. The 5th floor of the latter is occupied by the broadcasting station, Radio Clyde.

Ailsa Hypermarket in the centre is said to be the biggest shop in Glasgow and the centre lays claim to being the first in Britain outside of London to have a travelator instead of an escalator.

This building complex, which is possibly the biggest in Glasgow, also contains the Anderston Cross Bus Station. The Anderston Cross Centre was built on the site of old tenements and Pitt Street Lodging House.

The adjacent Argyle Street Car Park is built mainly on the site of Bishop Street, so named because it was formerly church land.

Opposite Anderston Cross Bus Station in Argyle Street is the new Glasgow Centre Hotel which was opened in 1975. It contains 126 bedrooms and has the unusual distinction of not having any right angles in its construction due to its peculiar alignment with James Watt Street.

Slightly to the north of the Anderston Centre is the largest post office building in Scotland, Dial House. Next is the Albany Hotel and lastly St Patrick's Roman Catholic Church, North Street.

Below to our left at 26–28 Washington Street we see the red sandstone building of the old Washington Street School built in 1890. For some years now it has been the premises of the Glasgow Art Centre, the only one of its kind in Glasgow.

To our right is the Daily Record Newspaper Building. It was opened by Her Royal Highness Princess Anne, on 26th November, 1971. It was the first paper in Scotland to produce newspapers in colour on its own premises.

On the other side of Kingston Bridge we enter the district of Kingston. Fixed on the wall of the under part of the bridge at this end is a large bronze plaque with the inscription.

Kingston Bridge
Opened by
Her Majesty Queen Elizabeth
The Queen Mother 26th June 1970.

To our left at Shearer Street is the site of the Kingston Dock, the oldest dock in Glasgow, where at one time the West Highland boats berthed and where general cargoes, including cement and china clay, were unloaded. Now the site is overrun with weeds and there is little to remind us that it ever was a dock, except for the old capstans that still line the edge of the old basin which has now been infilled.

Soon we pass the skilfully designed Scottish Co-operative Wholesale Society Buildings in Morrison Street known simply as the Co-op Buildings since the SCWS merged with the English Co-operative Wholesale Society in 1973. The main building is said to have been built to a rejected design submitted for the Glasgow City Chambers, an allegation which the architects hotly denied at the time.

To our right we observe Pollok Street, which was once the widest street in Glasgow. Before redevelopment at No. 3 Pollok Street stood Pollok Street Church of Scotland. It was built in 1855, the last service was conducted in the church on the 8th of June, 1975.

Weir Street Hall was used as a children's nursery by the church. It is said to have been the first children's nursery in Glasgow, possibly even Scotland, and served as a model for other nurseries to follow. The Corporation continued using the building as a nursery for a while before it was demolished.

At 348 Paisley Road is Kingston Hall built in 1903 and housing the local public library. The facade of the building is adorned with the Glasgow Coat of Arms, two medallions depicting the faces of two gentlemen and a full sized female statue holding a sheaf of papers. The latter no doubt represents learning.

To the rear of the Kingston Hall at Parkholm Lane are the former premises of Kingston Police Station complete with seven stoutly made prison cells, and if the walls could speak what a story they could tell! However, the old prison has since been taken over by a business firm and now the cells house nothing more turbulent than inanimate business materials.

At the General Terminus, Plantation Quay, could be seen huge iron-ore ships unloading cargoes of iron-ore ready to be sent by rail to Ravenscraig and the Clyde Iron Works. They disappeared when Hunterston came into operation. All that is left in this part of the Clyde is McBrayne's West Highland Cargo Steamer, *Loch Carron* and the Paddle Steamer *Waverley,* which leaves from the Waverley Terminal, Anderston Quay.

A pillar of stone with a plate bearing the number 288 in Paisley Road facing Weir Street is the only apparent relic left of the now demolished Eagle House that once belonged to Currie & Co. Ltd., building trade merchants. The stone eagle surmounting the house was a replica of the one perched on the Eagle Building in Bothwell Street. It has been said that this eagle represented a brand of cement from Germany used by Currie, and that earlier the house was used by the German Embassy.

Many of the old tenements in this area were demolished to make way for parkland. Mr Oldham, Glasgow's former Director of Parks received, in 1974, the St Mungo's Award of £1,000 for revolutionising the use of parks in Glasgow and making the city more attractive.

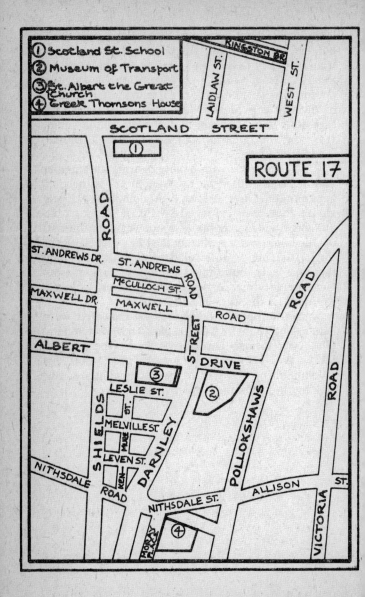

1. Scotland St. School
2. Museum of Transport
3. St. Albert the Great Church
4. Greek Thomsons House

KINGSTON BR.

LAIDLAW ST.

WEST ST.

SCOTLAND STREET

1

ROUTE 17

ST. ANDREWS DR.

ST. ANDREWS

ROAD

ROAD

McCULLOCH ST.

MAXWELL DR.

MAXWELL

ROAD

ALBERT

STREET DRIVE

ROAD

3

2

LESLIE ST.

ST.

SHIELDS

MELVILLE ST.

MURE ST.

DARNLEY

POLLOKSHAWS

LEVEN ST.

KEN ST.

NITHSDALE

ROAD

ROAD

NITHSDALE ST.

ALLISON

ST.

VICTORIA

4

MOSSPARK

88

Route 17

WEST STREET – SCOTLAND STREET – SHIELDS ROAD – ST ANDREW'S ROAD – DARNLEY STREET – NITHSDALE ROAD – NITHSDALE STREET

Moving straight on from Kingston Bridge we enter Carnoustie Street (prior to 1932 known as Crookston Street) and eventually arrive at Scotland Street.

At 195 Scotland Street are the huge premises of James Howden & Co Ltd, engineers, founded in 1854 by James Howden of Prestonpans. In 1882 Howden patented the Howden Hot Air Blast System which increased the efficiency of boilers. The firm is proud of the fact that they installed engines in such ships as the *Xanth* in 1869 and the *Queen Elizabeth* in 1872.

Close by, at 225 Scotland Street, is Scotland Street School. built in 1904 and designed by Charles Rennie Mackintosh, one of his most pleasing buildings.

Across the road from the school all the tenements have been demolished and all that now remains is the entrance to the Shields Road Subway Station, one of the fifteen subway stations in the city. The subway circuit can be travelled in 28 minutes and has recently been rebuilt under a modernisation plan.

Turning into Shields Road, the road that leads into Pollokshields and at one time one of the most fashionable areas in Glasgow, we observe on our right a huge building standing amid the demolished buildings like an oasis in the desert. The facade of this building at 401 Scotland Street is worthy of mention. It depicts four sculptured heads that appear to represent an Indian, a Negro, a Chinaman and a European, and also two lions and a bird that is possibly a griffin in the act of catching a snake. This building, belonging to Slater Rodger & Co., was built in 1904 and the items mentioned appear to symbolise the world-wide trading interests of the firm.

We now travel along Shields Road and cross the railway lines where once stood three railway stations, namely Pollokshields Station, Shields Road Station, and Shields Station which served the Glasgow and Paisley joint railways, Union Railway, South Western Railway and Caledonian Railway, long before they were formed into British Rail.

Still travelling up Shields Road, called after the lands of that name, we turn left at St Andrew's Road, the first thoroughfare to be built in Pollokshields. At this point, to our right, is the St Andrew's Drive Housing Scheme, built around 1969 and designed by the Glasgow City Architects comprising 560 houses contained in seven blocks each of eight storeys. It was built on the site of some former mansions and was the first major housing scheme in Pollokshields.

We now travel along St Andrew's Road which follows the curve of the old Glasgow, Paisley and Ardrossan Canal, now a railway track. The canal was started in 1816 but never finished. We then cross Maxwell Road, named after the Maxwells of Pollok, and there to our left are three huge gas holders which initially belonged to Tradeston Gas Works and were then taken over by Provan Gas Works. The Gas Board moved to this site on 15th June, 1975 from George Square.

In Darnley Street, between Maxwell Road and Albert Drive are a number of firms, and the premises of the publishing firm Miller and Lang were once here as well, in a building erected in 1902.

Continuing our journey along Darnley Street we soon arrive at Albert Drive and see the Museum of Transport which was opened by Her Majesty Queen Elizabeth the Queen Mother on 14th April, 1964, some time after the Glasgow trams were removed from service on 4th September, 1962.

In the museum can be seen a wide variety of transport vehicles, including Scottish Argyle cars dating back to 1900, and early steam locomotives that were built in the then world-renowned locomotive works at Springburn.

Also in Albert Drive, at the corner of Glenapp Street, is St Albert the Great Roman Catholic Church. This church was named after the Dominican friar Albertus Magnus, whereas Albert Drive itself was named after Queen Victoria's husband Prince Albert. Prior to being sold to the Catholic community this building was occupied by Stockwell Free Church later known as the Albert Drive Church.

We cross Albert Drive and turn left at Nithsdale Road to cross the railway bridge. On our right we pass what used to be the Strathbungo Railway Station booking offices. The station is now closed and the booking offices have been converted into shops.

Nearby is Fotheringay Road named after Fotheringay Castle where Mary Queen of Scots was executed. Her son James VI of Scotland later razed Fotheringay Castle to the ground, because his mother had been executed there.

Close by is Moray Place. Nos 1–10 were designed in 1859–60 by the famous architect Alexander Thomson known as 'Greek' Thomson. He resided for a while at No. 1 Moray Place but about seventy years ago No. 81 Nithsdale Road was added to this building as a surgery extension by a Dr Forrest. It is easy to see that the architect tried to copy the Thomson design but was not entirely successful. It is intended to raise a memorial on the adjacent traffic island to the memory of Greek Thomson. A competition for a suitable memorial was sponsored by the New Glasgow Society and won by Mr Fred Selby, an architect who lives in the area.

Passing down Nithsdale Street, we see situated at No. 43, one of the last remaining sandstone houses of the village of Strathbungo. Nearby is March Street and at No. 22 are the old premises of the Strathbungo Police Station. At the corner of Pollokshaws Road and Nithsdale Street are five trees where the oldest house in Strathbungo used to be.

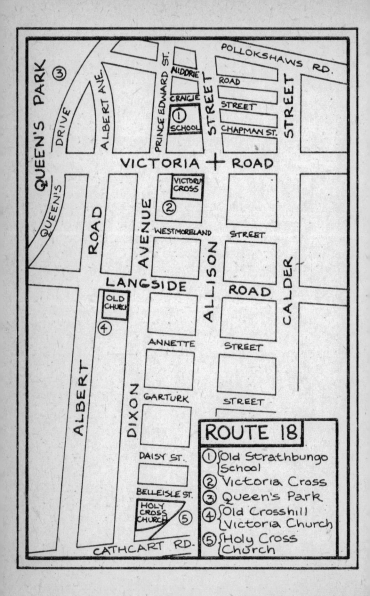

POLLOKSHAWS RD.

QUEEN'S PARK ③

ALBERT AVE.

DRIVE

QUEEN'S

PRINCE EDWARD ST.

NIDDRIE

CRAIGIE

SCHOOL ①

STREET

ROAD

STREET

CHAPMAN ST.

STREET

VICTORIA ✚ ROAD

VICTORIA CROSS ②

ROAD

AVENUE

WESTMORELAND

STREET

LANGSIDE

OLD CHURCH

④

ALLISON ROAD

CALDER

ANNETTE

STREET

ALBERT

DIXON

GARTURK

STREET

DAISY ST.

BELLEISLE ST.

HOLY CROSS CHURCH ⑤

CATHCART RD.

ROUTE 18

① Old Strathbungo School
② Victoria Cross
③ Queen's Park
④ Old Crosshill Victoria Church
⑤ Holy Cross Church

94

Route 18

ALLISON STREET – VICTORIA ROAD – DIXON AVENUE

We cross Pollokshaws Road and enter Allison Street, which was formerly the dividing line between Renfrewshire and Lanarkshire, but is now in the County of Glasgow.

The Police Station at 86 Craigie Street was built in 1896. The Glasgow Coat of Arms is cut on the facade.

Across from here is Strathbungo School. Chiselled on the facade of the building are its name and the date of its erection (1894) in Roman numerals.

The old Strathbungo Higher Grade 1914–18 War Memorial can still be seen. On it is the unusual epitaph

These laid the world away,
Poured out the red wine of youth

followed by 96 names.

We now turn right into Victoria Road. This crossing is known as Victoria Cross, as indicated by the large gold painted wrought iron letters that adorn the highest corner at the crossing. Below this sign on the ground floor was the provision shop of James and George Hunter. It was a James Hunter of this family who was the last Provost of Crosshill in 1890–91 before Crosshill and Govanhill were annexed to Glasgow.

Proceeding along Victoria Road, that perpetuates the memory of Queen Victoria, we find this road a splendid shopping centre and something akin to Byres Road in the West End of the city.

According to the records, Crosshill to the south was named after an ancient cross that once stood on the summit of a hill, probably at the highest part of Queen Mary Avenue. The cross was about ten feet high and three and a half feet wide and carved on it was Christ entering Jerusalem riding an ass. However, religious fanatics completely destroyed it.

Facing us are the main gates of the beautiful Queen's Park, part of which was originally the Pathhead Farm and acquired in 1857 from Mr Neale Thomson of Camphill at a cost of £30,000. In 1893 the adjoining estate of Camphill was bought by the city at a cost of £63,000. The park occupies 148 acres and is named after Mary Queen of Scots who lost the Battle of Langside near this area in 1568.

We turn left at Dixon Avenue, that keeps alive the memory of William Dixon, the noted iron and coal master who came from Newcastle in 1771 and eventually bought the estate of Govanhill, principally for the potential mineral wealth that lay beneath the surface of the area. Many productive coal pits were therefore opened here and many of the thoroughfares in this area have names to do with him and his family. Belleisle Street keeps alive the memory of his residence of that name in Ayrshire and Calder Street commemorates the Calder Iron Works, in Old Monkland, Lanarkshire, which he acquired in 1805. It has also been suggested that the Allison, Annette and Daisy Streets were named after his three daughters.

At the corner of Langside Road is the old Crosshill Victoria Church now being used as an art centre. Crosshill Victoria Church was initially founded as Crosshill Church. Later it united with Victoria Church from Eglinton Toll, and in 1974 it united with Queen's Park High Parish Church in Queen's Drive.

Langside Road was originally known as Pathhead Road and led past Pathhead Farmhouse, the grounds of which have since been formed into Queen's Park. The old farmhouse still stands near the top of the granite steps in Queen's Park and now serves as the Queen's Park Superintendent's house.

As we travel along Dixon Avenue we notice the fine turreted terraced houses, quite an unusual feature in this area and an indication of the time they were built. The date 1905 is cut on a stone on the facade of the house at No. 40.

Passing by Annette Street we are reminded that Arthur Whitten Brown, one of the first men to fly across the Atlantic, once lived here at No. 42. Brown and his partner John Alcock used a Vickers Vimy aeroplane and completed their journey in 16 hours and 27 minutes. Later they were knighted.

At the corner of Belleisle Street and Dixon Avenue is the Holy Cross Roman Catholic Church built in 1911. The original Holy Cross Chapel School was built in 1882 in Daisy Street. It still stands and it was the first Catholic Church to be built in this area. In 1900 another chapel school was built adjacent to the original, and it also is standing and in use.

It has been said that the tenement building beside the church and the school at No. 34 Daisy Street was built from stones from the demolished Port Eglinton Barracks in Eglinton Street.

A link with the old Burgh of Crosshill is established when we look at the old wooden building at Number 19A Belleisle Street. This was the site of the Burgh of Crosshill Fire Station, and adjacent to it at No. 21 are the police station and court rooms with a date that looks like 1881 cut on the stone above the door. At No. 23 are the old police dwelling houses that are still in use.

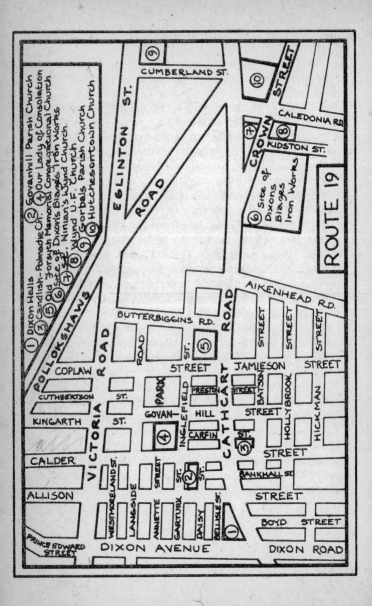

ROUTE 19

① Dixon Halls
② Candlish-Polmadie Ch.
③ Old Gorbals Memorial Congregational Church
④ Our Lady of Consolation Church
⑤ Site of Dixon's Blazes Iron Works
⑥ St. Ninian's Wynd Church
⑦ Wynd U.F. Church
⑧ Govanhill Parish Church
⑨ Gorbals Parish Church
⑩ Hutchesontown Church

CUMBERLAND ST.

EGLINTON STREET

ROAD

CALEDONIA RD.

CROWN STREET

KIDSTON ST.

⑥ Site of Dixon's Blazes Iron Works

AIKENHEAD RD.

BUTTERBIGGINS RD.

POLLOKSHAWS ROAD

VICTORIA ROAD

CATHCART ROAD

COPLAW STREET

JAMIESON STREET

ROAD

STREET

CUTHBERTSON ST.

PARK

INGLEFIELD

PRESTON

BATSON STREET

HOLLYBROOK STREET

HICKMAN STREET

KINGARTH ST.

GOVAN

HILL

CARFIN

STREET

CALDER

ST.

STREET

ALLISON

WESTMORELAND ST.

LANGSIDE

ANNETTE STREET

GARTURK ST.

DAISY ST.

DELISLE ST.

BANKHALL ST.

STREET

DIXON AVENUE

BOYD STREET

DIXON ROAD

PRINCE EDWARD STREET

98

Route 19

CATHCART ROAD

At the corner of Dixon Avenue and Cathcart Road we see Dixon Halls built on the boundary between Crosshill and Govanhill and partly in one district and partly in the other. There is a memorial slab inside which indicates that the building was erected by William Smith Dixon for the joint use of Crosshill and Govanhill and opened on 12th September, 1879. The slab was put up by Govan Colliery.

On the facade of the Dixon Halls are three finely cut sculptured heads and above the entrance is cut the armorial bearings of William Smith Dixon with the motto *Fortes, Fortuna, Juvat,* and the initials W.S.D. In common with most of the buildings in the area, Dixon Halls is mainly built of Giffnock stone from the old Giffnock Quarries.

After Cathcart Road, Dixon Avenue becomes Dixon Road, and were we to proceed along this road we would reach first Aikenhead Road and then Polmadie Road where the Polmadie Refuse Disposal Works opened in December 1958 are situated. They are one of the largest in Britain and take care of half the city's refuse.

Polmadie is an area that has associations with Mary Queen of Scots. Legend has it that when the Queen fled from the Battle of Langside she was riding her favourite horse Paul. The horse, however, fell and had to be destroyed, and the Queen supposedly said, 'Poll may dee that I may flee'. Thus, it is argued, was born the name 'Polmadie'. In actual fact, though, 'Polmadie' comes from a Gaelic word meaning the stream or pool haunted by wolves.

Instead of proceeding to Polmadie, however, we turn left at Cathcart Road. At the corner of Cathcart

Road and Allison Street once stood Govanhill Parish Church popularly known as the Cathedral. It was demolished on 29th May, 1975. However, before this, the congregation had united with Govanhill Church of Scotland, Daisy Street.

The 1914–18 war memorial from the old Govanhill Parish Church now stands at this new location and serves as a lasting link with the church and also keeps alive the memory of the 50 men of the congregation who fell in the Great War.

Next we come to Bankhall Street named after Bankhall House which formerly stood near here. Further on, at the corner of Cathcart Road and Calder Street stands what used to be Candlish Memorial Church. This church was built in 1874, and in 1967 it united with Polmadie Church. It is now known as the Candlish-Polmadie Church of Scotland.

It has been proposed to demolish the old picture houses and adjoining tenements in Calder Street in order to lay out a football pitch for the neighbouring Holy Cross Primary School which was built in 1914 and originally known as the Calder Street School.

The former Chairman of the British Steel Corporation, Harold Montague Finniston, was born at Polmadie and educated at Allan Glen's School.

Still travelling along Cathcart Road we come to Carfin Street, and we see situated in Inglefield Street and facing up Carfin Street, the new Roman Catholic Church, Our Lady of Consolation, opened in 1971 by the Archbishop of Glasgow.

The church is built on the site of the old Majestic Picture House known locally as the Magic Stick. This was the first picture house to be erected in this area. In the days before the advent of the talkies it cost only a penny to attend the children's matinee. The show consisted of two full length features and a comedy, and was enthusiastically supported by an orchestra.

Shortly we come to Govanhill Street, which was formed on the lands of that name. Prior to 1877 Govanhill District was known as 'No Man's Land', because it lay between Glasgow and the Burgh of Crosshill. Both towns wanted to annex this territory, but at that time their efforts were of no avail because Govanhill was made a burgh in 1877. Later, however, ironically, both Crosshill and Govanhill were annexed to Glasgow in 1891.

Looking down Preston Street we see the four acre Govanhill Park situated in Inglefield Street. It was acquired in 1896 and was originally a brickfield.

Passing Coplaw Street we see the red sandstone Forsyth Memorial Congregational Church at 147–149 Coplaw Street. A memorial stone on the facade of the church reads:–

5th September 1903
Memorial Stone
Laid by
Mrs Hickman Morgan
of
Govanhill.

Mrs Hickman Morgan gave her name to Hickman Street and Morgan Street, and was the founder of the Mary Morgan Trust. She was a member of the Dixon family.

Walking up Cathcart Road it was once possible to see the Pinkston Cooling Tower situated on a hill in the distance. Not many people knew it stood on an island surrounded by the waters of the Forth and Clyde Canal. Since then the tower has been demolished.

Butterbiggins Road which we arrive at next, is called after a country estate by this name that once existed in this area, and, similarly, Inglefield Street and Larkfield Street were named after estates in the vicinity.

We are now entering the area of Gorbals which forms part of the Queen's Park Parliamentary Constituency.

Gorbals was once part of the Parish of Govan, but the Barony of Gorbals was made a parish of its own in 1771. The area was then only 28½ acres but has been added to the city since 1846.

Soon we arrive at the junction of Cathcart Road and Crown Street. In Crown Street, at this point, is the site of the old Dixon's Blazes Iron Works that was a famous landmark by virtue of the perpetual lurid flames issuing from the six furnaces.

It was here that Sir Henry Bessemer who was born in 1813 and died in 1898, carried out his earliest experiments. He was the son of a Huguenot and invented a superior type of steel called Bessemer steel which was widely used on railings and other projects where great tenacity and tensile strength are required. He was knighted in 1879. The site comprising 35 acres was purchased by Templeton for a carpet factory in 1961. Since then carpets from this factory have already carpeted the House of Lords, the House of Commons and the banqueting hall of the Glasgow City Chambers. The company was formed by James Templeton in 1839.

Opposite Templeton's Carpet Factory and facing the junction is the tastefully designed St Ninian's Wynd Church which has now been closed. Scanning the facade of this red sandstone building it is possible to see three memorial stones laid during its foundation in 1888, the first by J. C. White, Esquire, the second by Rev. J. B. Wilson, D.D., and the third by Mrs Still, a noted benefactress of the church. The church building is quite unusual in that above the main entrance are the following words cut in the stone, 'Worthy is the Lamb' and cut above the entrance to the manse are the words 'Jehovah

Shalom', which evidently means 'The Peace of God Be on You'. Unfortunately this fine church may be demolished as it is in the path of a proposed roadway.

Diagonally across Crown Street stands the Wynd United Free Church which will be retained. To reinstate it in another area would cost from a quarter to half a million pounds. It will form the nucleus of the proposed Gorbals Park whose boundaries will extend from Cathcart Road to Lawmoor Street and from Caledonia Road to Templeton's Carpet Factory. Nearby is old Camden Street School and this area will be included in the park as well.

At the corner of Cathcart Road and Caledonia Road is another closed church. This was designed by Greek Thomson, and although now little more than a shell, still retains some of its former beauty.

Soon we arrive at Cumberland Street named after the Duke of Cumberland who fought against Bonnie Prince Charlie at the Battle of Culloden on 16th April 1746. It was the last battle to be fought on British Soil.

We are now in Gorbals Street. Alas, though, old Gorbals has practically passed away except for a few of the old tenements now lying stark and empty, with window panes smashed and the fitments from the interiors of the houses ruthlessly ripped from their sockets by vandals. The bulldozers will soon raze to the ground the sturdy old sandstone buildings which served the district for well over a hundred years.

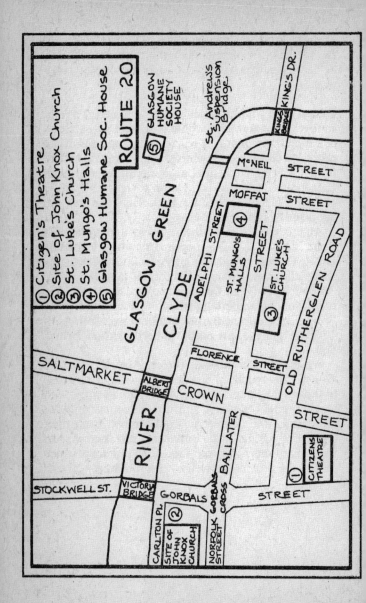

ROUTE 20

① Citizen's Theatre
② Site of John Knox Church
③ St. Luke's Church
④ St. Mungo's Halls
⑤ Glasgow Humane Soc. House

⑤ GLASGOW HUMANE SOCIETY HOUSE

KING'S DR.

KINGS BRIDGE

St. Andrew's Suspension Bridge

McNEIL STREET

MOFFAT STREET

GLASGOW GREEN

ADELPHI STREET

④

ST. MUNGO'S HALLS

STREET

③ ST. LUKE'S CHURCH

CLYDE

OLD RUTHERGLEN ROAD

FLORENCE STREET

SALTMARKET

ALBERT BRIDGE

CROWN STREET

RIVER

BALLATER STREET

① CITIZENS THEATRE

STOCKWELL ST.

VICTORIA BRIDGE

GORBALS STREET

GORBALS CROSS

CARLTON PL.

② SITE OF JOHN KNOX CHURCH

NORFOLK STREET

Route 20

GORBALS STREET –
BALLATER STREET

The Gorbals Swimming Baths at 146 Gorbals Street are now closed. They were built on ground costing £3 10s. per square yard and opened in 1885. They were the second oldest baths on the south side of the city. Inside the main entrance was a brass war memorial to the seventeen members of the South Side Amateur Swimming Club who were killed in the 1914–18 war.

Also the two flats above the shops in this building were in the early days used in connection with the Art Galleries and Museum for exhibition purposes.

At No. 150 was the public library and the lettering 'Public Library' can still be seen above the door. The premises have now been taken over to serve as the Talbot Association for the underprivileged, who are mostly alcoholics. The Association is named in honour of Matt Talbot, a Dublin man, born in 1856, who was an extreme alcoholic and who, with great perseverance, managed to overcome his addiction. It was opened around 1973.

Across the road from the Gorbals Swimming Baths is the Citizens' Theatre where there were six statues surmounting the edifice and representing Robert Burns, Shakespeare and the Muses. These statues were taken down in July 1977. The Citizens' Theatre was originally the Princess's Theatre, where such well known actors as Tommy Lorne and George West starred in the old days. A treasured relic of the theatre is a statuette of the late Duncan McRae which is a replica of the one in the Glasgow Art Galleries. There is also an oil painting of McRae taken in the costume of Jamie the Scot, the title of a play he acted in. It is said there are very few paintings of actors taken while wearing their acting apparel.

There are two plaques in the entrance hall which read as follows:–

1) Osborne Henry Mavor
   James Bridie
   C.B.E., L.L.D., M.D., F.R.F.P.S., (G)
   Physician, Dramatist.
   1888–1951

2) This Theatre
   came into the possession of
   Richard Waldon
   1886.
   Directed and Managed by
   him until his death.
   1922.

Both the bronze plaques are adorned with likenesses of their subjects.

Beside the Citizens' Theatre was the Old Palace Picture House which was latterly a bingo hall and adjacent to this building at one time were the National Halls. Although the Citizens' Theatre is a listed building there was talk of demolishing it some years ago due largely to the rising costs of maintaining a stone building and the great shortage of stone masons to carry out the work. The Citizens' Theatre has since been reprieved.

Gorbals Cross has undergone sweeping changes. The last remaining old tenement at the cross was demolished on 23rd July, 1975. Some of the stones were taken from the site to reinforce the embankment around the Queen's Park flagpole. This building had the words 'Elphinstone Place' on it and was the last remaining link in Gorbals with the Elphinstone Mansion which stood at one time at the corner of Gorbals Street and Rutherglen Road and features largely in old pictures of the village of Gorbals. The Mansion was the home of Sir George Elphinstone, Provost of Glasgow in 1605.

The Muslim Mission which once stood in nearby Oxford Street has been demolished as well. I wondered for a long time where all the massive stones from the building had gone, but then the mystery was solved unexpectedly one day when I was walking by the Duck Pond in Queen's Park. A pile of sandstone blocks fresh from some building site lay in heaps around the pond ready to be used to reinforce its embankment. The foreman employed on the work informed me that he thought the stones came from some Masonic Hall as there were Masonic symbols painted on several of them. However, on inspection I found to my surprise, that they were none other than the painted stones complete with the Muslim Crescent and Star from the demolished Muslim Mission in Oxford Street.

The Mission's mosque is now at 61 Carlton Place which runs parallel to Oxford Street. Near here were once the Gorbals Primary School and Gorbals Parish Church. These, however, were demolished in 1975, and the site will be used to build a Sherrif Court Complex.

To all appearances this area is a ghost town with here and there an oasis of fresh construction and activity with perhaps the promise of better things to come.

Many of the buildings and streets prior to demolition have wisely been photographed by far-seeing citizens, perhaps because a series of street scenes of old Glasgow, taken in the 1860's by photographer Thomas Annan, were sold for £7,500 at Sotheby's in London in 1974.

At the corner of Thistle Street and Ballater Street was the old Cunningham Church, where the Rev.

Cameron Peddie once served. He was a noted faith healer and took an interest in the local gangs such as the Bee Hive, South Side Stickers and Coburg Erin, founding a club to keep them off the streets. This church burned down and was demolished in 1978.

Florence Street, which is also in this area, was once called Rose Street, and Camden Street was called Shamrock Street. Together with Thistle Street, these represented the three united countries, and the nearby Crown Street represented the ruling monarch. When Gorbals was annexed to Glasgow some street names had to be changed to avoid duplicating names already existing in the city.

Crossing Crown Street we observe to our left the College of Nautical Studies where 250 cadets from all parts of the world are trained every year for the Merchant Navy. This college often has the highest pass marks for the Merchant Navy in all Britain.

Several decades ago, Gorbals was densely populated and the youths weren't as affluent as the youths of today, so they had to make their own entertainment and make it as cheaply as possible. Consequently many football teams sprang up which required very little financial expenditure. The teams formed generally took the name of the street or district they were drawn from and included Commercial Athletic Juvenile team from around Commercial Road, who wore green and white jerseys – Hutchesontown Athletic Juvenile team from around Surrey Street and Portugal Street – Stafford Juvenile team, and Fernhill Juvenile team from Orchard Street.

One team of particular interest was the Rancel Secondary Juvenile team drawn from around Cumberland Street and Surrey street. They sometimes wore old blue or green jerseys. As the reader has perhaps guessed, their name was a combination of the first three letters of Rangers and Celtic. In other words, they attempted to be as impartial to both teams as possible.

They were highly successful and won all honours in Glasgow's Secondary Juvenile League including the Lady Darling National Cup. Like all the teams mentioned, they are now defunct.

St Luke's Roman Catholic Church in Ballater Street was opened on 27th April 1975. The architect was William J. Gilmour, and it seats 350 people. Next to the church is St Luke's School and Boys' Guild Hall. Benny Lynch, flyweight boxer and Scotland's first world champion, was born at 17 Florence Street in 1913. He often sparred in the hall.

Among the pupils who attended the St Luke's School or were associated with the Boys' Guild Hall, were Jim McCalliog who played football for Southampton and Paddy Crerand who played for Manchester United. During the last war James Stokes of the King's Shropshire Light Infantry won the V.C. posthumously in 1945 while in action at Kervenheim, Holland.

Continuing our journey along Ballater Street we come to Ballater Place. It is said that this is the only housing scheme in Britain that was built without one single window pane being broken. Situated at a gable end in this scheme and attached to the wall is a small plaque that states

Commended
for
Good Design
by the
Saltire Society
1958.

Directly to the south of this scheme are the tall housing blocks of Queen Elizabeth Square. Attached to the wall of one of the blocks is a memorial that has inscribed on it: 'This memorial stone was unveiled by Her Majesty Queen Elizabeth on the occasion of her visit here on 30th June 1961'.

A little further on are the four multi-storey blocks of Waddell Court and Commercial Court that were opened around 1963 and built on the site of buildings at Waddell Street and Commercial Road that had been previously demolished.

Soon we pass Moffat Street where stands the fine red sandstone edifice of the Co-operative St Mungo Halls, appropriately surmounted by a large statue thought to be that of St Mungo. Cut on the facade of the building is the date 1905. It has been closed since 1973 as it is considered too costly to run. The St Mungo Halls, prior to the Scottish Co-operative Society's merger with the English Co-operative Society on 12th May, 1973, were used for all types of functions.

At McNeil Street the St Andrew's Suspension Bridge spans the River Clyde and leads on to the Glasgow Green and the Glasgow Humane Society House. It is on record that the officers of the Society have recovered from the River Clyde and surrounding waterways more than 500 bodies within the last eighty years and rescued more than 1,000 people.

Also in Ballater Street, in this immediate area, are several distilleries including Kingarth Strathclyde and Black and White which together export millions of gallons of whisky to all corners of the world.

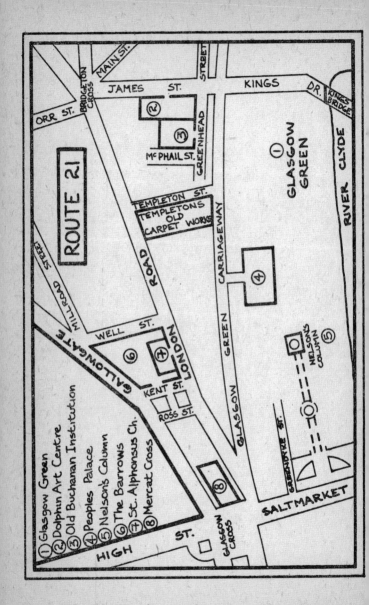

Route 21

KING'S BRIDGE – KING'S DRIVE – GLASGOW GREEN CARRIAGEWAY – LONDON ROAD

We now proceed to King's Bridge and once again cross the Clyde, which at this point seems unusually clear and is reminiscent of a rural scene as it meanders along, skirting the south side of Glasgow Green. It was on Glasgow Green that traditional showmen like Cadona, Taylor, White, Wilmot and Evans once performed.

Turning left at Glasgow Green Carriageway beside Greenhead Street we now skirt the northern border of Glasgow Green. At the corner of Greenhead Street and James Street is the Dolphin Arts Centre used by the Strathclyde Region Education Department. In 1978 the first city farm was started here and bee hives were installed on the roof. The 1978 harvest was a hundred pounds of pure honey. Formerly this building was occupied by Logan and Johnston's School of Domestic Economy used for training nurses, and a stone on the face of the building left from that time has a bee hive on it and the date 1890.

The bee hive is indicative of work, obedience, diligence, creative ability and wealth. There was also a bee hive stone above the main entrance of Gorbals Primary School in Carlton Place which was demolished in 1975. The bee hive seems an apt symbol and sets a worthy example for the pupils of any school to follow.

Next to Logan and Johnston's School at No. 47 Greenhead Street was Fairfield Day Centre for Children, now Greenview Special School. Prior to 1974 it was known as St Aidan's School, but originally housed the Buchanan Institution, founded in 1859 through a bequest to the City by Mr James Buchanan for the benefit of destitute boys. Mr Buchanan had interests in the West Indies. The stone figure of a boy reading a book surmounts the building, and represents one of the destitute boys. There are some fine stained glass windows, including one with the apt motto 'Do Good'.

The building at 12 Greenhead Street serves as a reminder of Glasgow's shipping past as it was once a home for Lascar seamen. Since the decline in shipping in Glasgow, the Lascar seamen who came from India and were employed as deck hands on coastal and ocean going liners have virtually disappeared from the streets of Glasgow.

Skirting the north side of Glasgow Green and travelling along Greenhead Street, we come to Templeton Street where at one time stood the Greenhead Swimming Pond and Washhouse. The site of the baths is now covered by an extension to Templeton's Carpet Works.

The facade of Templeton's Carpet Works is designed after the style of the Doge's Palace in Venice. It collapsed on 1st November, 1889 during its construction killing 29 women who were within the adjacent weaving sheds. However, it was finally finished in 1892 and the firm moved here from their original premises in King Street (now Redan Street), Bridgeton. The building is currently used for storage by both them and other companies.

Facing here, on Glasgow Green, can be seen 33 evenly spaced iron posts that served as a drying green. It was once used by women who washed their clothes in the Greenhead Washhouse and by the maids of the wealthy people who resided in nearby Monteith Row and round about. It is still used today by the local people, but much less frequently.

Soon we arrive at the People's Palace Museum, a fine red sandstone building erected in 1894, which displays items of special interest about Glasgow.

At the back of the People's Palace there is a fountain in memory of Hugh McDonald (1817–60), poet and author of 'Rambles Round Glasgow' and 'Days At The Coast', with a stanza of verse that runs thus,

> The Bonnie Wee Well on the Breist of the Brae
> Where the hare steals to drink in the Gloamin sae Grey
> Where the wild moorland hen dips her neb and tak's wing
> And the Lark weets his whistle ere Mounting to sing.

Hugh McDonald is buried in the Southern Necropolis, Caledonia Road.

A prominent landmark on the Green is Nelson's Column, erected in 1807 and the first in Britain. It commemorates Nelson's famous victories Aboukir (1798), Copenhagen (1801), St Vincent (1797), and Trafalgar (1805).

Near Nelson's Column is a huge boulder and it is inscibed as follows

> Near this spot in 1765
> James Watt conceived the
> idea of the separate
> condenser for the steam
> engine patented, 1769

Facing the People's Palace is a beautiful wrought iron fountain manufactured by Walter McFarlane & Co. in their Saracen Foundry in Possilpark.

Glasgow Green is part of the old Bishop's Forest that once almost encircled Glasgow. The Bishop used to hunt wild boar and red deer in medieval times. It is said that Glasgow Green is the oldest park in Europe and it is certainly the oldest in Glasgow.

Skirting Glasgow Green at this point we are running parallel with the once fashionable Monteith Row. In 1819 plans were drawn up to erect Monteith Row and it was named in honour of Henry Monteith who was Provost of the City and one of the merchant princes connected with the Turkey-Red dyeing process.

Alas, Monteith Row has fallen on bad times. The wealthy people who were once residents have long since moved away, and most of the row is now demolished and has become run down and sleazy.

The Green in front of Monteith Row has become the happy hunting ground of the underprivileged, many of them alcoholics and drug addicts who seem to have little hope of a proper existence. The surrounding area emits an atmosphere of decay and wantonness, although an incongruous touch is manifested by the stately and luxuriantly green trees and well-kept gardens of the Green which contrast vividly with the decrepit and ill-kept tenements.

As we enter London Road, to our right, centred around Kent Street, Stevenson Street and Moncur Street, is Glasgow's famous market, the 'Barrows'. There is a large sign over an entrance to the Barrows in London Road which reads 'Alight Here For Barrowland', and hundreds of thousands come here for bargains from all parts of Scotland.

Barrowland was started by Mrs Margaret McIver in 1888 in a small fruit shop in Main Street, Bridgeton. She promoted business by hiring barrows at 1/6d a week. The present Barrowland Dance Hall was acquired in 1920. The Barrowland was opened in 1934 and was considered the most popular in Scotland. It was burned to the ground in 1958 and was rebuilt in 1964. Many famous people visited the hall including Henry Hall, Ray Fox, Teddy Joyce, Billy Tennent and Jack Hylton.

It is said Barrowland is changing its style and getting into the supermarket class but at one time it sold old clothes and other second hand items. Watches, cutlery, old books and carpets are sold here.

Near the Barrows in London Road is St Alphonsus Roman Catholic Church, and directly across the road, at 216–230 London Road, is the old St James Church with the date 1816.

Ross Street runs beside the Barrows, and at the corner of London Road and Ross Street is the Old Barns Public House. Nearby at one time stood a very narrow street known as Balaams Pass, where around 1920 Post Office workers, excavating the road discovered a cavalry sword, military buttons and other accoutrements.

Walking along London Road we arrive at Charlotte Street. It was previously called Merkdaily meaning a daily market where fruit and vegetables were sold. David Dale, Glasgow merchant and banker, and founder of the New Lanark Mills, had a house here which was later demolished to make way for a school extension.

At the end of Charlotte Street there is another entrance to Glasgow Green through an ornate archway which appears to the observer to be built the wrong way round.

A number of old buildings that may have been built around the same time as David Dale's house survive although in a very dilapidated state. Many of the houses in this street are said to have been designed by Robert Adam, the noted architect, and possibly some of these remaining houses are his handiwork.

It was at No. 30 Charlotte Street that John Stuart Blackie was born in 1809. A Scottish scholar, he published a translation of *Faust* and did a great deal to further the study of the Gaelic language.

Next is Moir Street, named after Bailie James Moir who was much abused because he advocated the building of street lavatories in the city. He lived to see his ideas carried out in all principal cities in Europe. He died in 1880, bequeathing all his valuable library to Glasgow and also £11,000 to buy books for the Mitchell Library. James Morrison Street nearby was named after another popular Bailie.

Many of the fine buildings in London Road have gone. An impressive sandstone building stands at the corner of Moir Street, but that is condemned too. As a result the tenants pay no rent or taxes – they only pay for gas and electricity. The Schipka Pass that used to be between London Road and the Gallowgate has been partly demolished as well. This took its name from a war fought between the Russians and the Turks. Local people were so impressed by this war that from then on it was called Schipka Pass. The official name was Gilmour Place.

Arriving back at the Tolbooth Steeple we look at the Mercat Cross again and we see cut on the stone the coat of arms of Glasgow's former Highland Light Infantry Regiment and their motto 'Nemo Me Impune Lacessit', which simply means 'Wha Daur Meddle Wi' Me'. The Highland Light Infantry amalgamated in 1959 with the Royal Scots Fusiliers to form the Royal Highland Fusiliers. It had 194 battle honours, more than any other regiment in Britain, and was the oldest regiment in Glasgow.

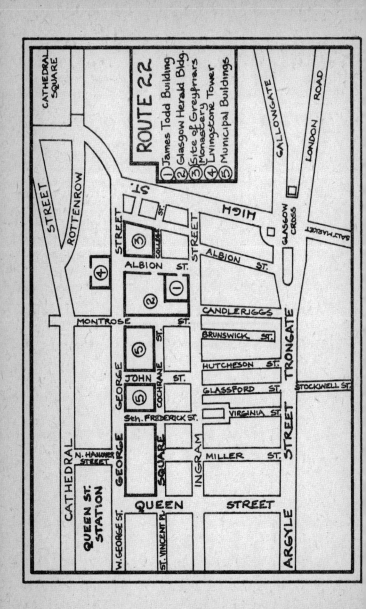

Route 22

GLASGOW CROSS – HIGH STREET – INGRAM STREET – ALBION STREET – GEORGE STREET – GEORGE SQUARE – NORTH HANOVER STREET

Turning into High Street at Glasgow Cross we notice there are six roads leading off the cross which makes it one of the busiest intersections in Glasgow. Included among the roads is the historical Gallowgate which once led out to a section of waste ground known as the Gallowmuir where criminals were executed.

It is said that the Coat of Arms of Scotland from the period before the Union was salvaged from the 2nd floor of the Tolbooth before it was demolished, and inserted for safe custody in the wall of a building in 7 High Street. This building has been demolished.

Proceeding up High Street we see on our left at 137 a five-storey red sandstone building extending into Bell Street. Although the design of the building is simple, the simplicity has been cleverly relieved by adornment at third floor level, and evenly spaced around the building are 13 lion heads cut on the stone.

At 97 High Street, near Blackfriars Street, is a fine grey sandstone building with fluted columns and the date 1893 cut on the facade.

At 123 High Street is another five-storey building now housing the A and B Divisions of the Glasgow Fire Prevention. A large Glasgow Coat of Arms is cut at the top of the face of the building, indicating that it was built as Corporation premises.

We now turn left into Ingram Street. The old tenements in Shuttle Street are all gone. The Foulis Brothers who lie buried underneath the pavement in

Ingram Street beside Ramshorn Church had a printing press there at one time. The ground floor premises were mainly used as an overflow from the old Fruit Market when it was in Candleriggs.

Turning right from Ingram Street into Albion Street, on our left, at 131 Albion Street, we see the James P. Todd Building. Also in Albion Street are the offices of the *Glasgow Herald*. These belonged briefly to the *Scottish Daily News* run under the workers' control from 5th May to 7th November, 1975, and before that they were occupied jointly by the *Glasgow Evening Citizen* and the *Scottish Sunday Express,* the former of which ceased publication in 1974 and the latter of which moved to Manchester.

In the entrance hall is a large mural depicting Trongate as it was many years ago. This building designed by Sir E. Owen Williams of London is listed to be preserved, chiefly because it is coated with Xylonite, a special material composed of sawdust mixed with Sorel cement.

It was at 203–213 Albion Street that the Glasgow Salvage Corps was founded in 1847. In 1972 they moved to their new £250,000 Salvage Corps Headquarters at 90 Maitland Street. This is also the street where the Glasgow Fair was started by the Greyfriars Monks who had a monastery here. The Greyfriars Church of Scotland was built in 1820 on its site and while digging the foundations hundreds of skeletons were discovered of young men with perfect teeth buried in a former graveyard attached to the monastery. It was rather puzzling why so many young men were buried in this place. It is known however that the new Greyfriars Church was replacing a former church built in 1742 in Shuttle Street and that many of the men of the Shuttle Street congregation volunteered to fight against Bonnie Prince Charlie at the Battle of Falkirk in 1746. The Glasgow volunteers suffered heavy losses and it is quite logical that they would be buried in the Greyfriars Churchyard in Albion Street, which was adjacent to their church.

In 1969 a dig was carried out on the site of the old Greyfriars Monastery. In the foundations were discovered fragments of old pottery.

Leaving Albion Street we turn left into George Street and at this point we observe Marland House at 40 George Street which house many Government Departments.

In this area was Tarbet Street which, in common with many other streets has been swept away by redevelopment. Miss Tarbet, whom it was named after, was a sister of Mrs Balmano who gave her name to Balmano Street.

Marland House is built astride Balmano Street, which was one of the steepest 'braes' in Glasgow and was used for many years for cycle races.

Directly in front of us is Livingstone Tower originally built as office blocks and now forming part of Strathclyde University. As the name implies, it was called after David Livingstone, the missionary and explorer.

In the vestibule of Livingstone Tower is a group fashioned in bronze representing Livingstone's famous 'last journey' when the dead missionary was carried 1,500 miles across Africa by a group of natives. The group is a copy of a carving in oak by Mr C. D. O. Pilkington and is a reminder of the time David Livingstone studied at Anderson College.

At the corner of Montrose Street and George Street built into the wall, is a foundation stone that states:–

This stone was laid by
His Majesty King Edward VII
14th May 1903.

At 63 John Street was the house where Lord Clyde was born. He has a statue erected to his memory in George Square. His house was demolished in 1975.

On our left hand side is the vast splendid edifice of the City Chambers which were designed by Mr William Young and opened by Queen Victoria in 1888. They are said to have the finest marble staircase in Europe, even finer than the one in the Vatican in Rome.

Just before entering George Square, at 266 George Street, is the old Parish Council building. Above the door are the words 'Parish Council', the Glasgow Coat of Arms and the motto *Protecere et Sustinere* meaning to protect and sustain. It is a fine doorway surmounted by two embossed reclining female figures supported by granite pillars. The adjacent building at 280 George Street has sculptured on the stone above the door the Royal Coat of Arms indicating a Government Building.

It may seem mundane to mention these sculptured Coats of Arms, but let us treasure these works of art, for in modern times it could be extremely difficult to get craftsmen to repeat them quite apart from the immense cost of doing so.

George Square has 12 statues and five of them represent Glasgow men, namely Lord Clyde, Thomas Graham, Sir John Moore, Thomas Campbell and James Oswald.

The Square was opened in 1787 and named in honour of King George III, and it was intended that his statue would be erected in the centre, but the statue of Sir Walter Scott now stands there instead.

The buildings on the north side of the Square are built on the original north bank of the River Clyde. In other words, the Square was part of the basin of the river. It is on record that the Municipal Buildings are built on a foundation of 40 feet of pure white sand.

124

Finally we are back at our starting place in North Hanover Street.

Most of us have been unexpectedly thrilled by the wealth of interest Glasgow has to offer and might even think back to the time when Daniel Defoe (1659–1731), who was sent to Scotland as a secret agent, stated that Glasgow was one of the cleanest, most beautiful and best-built cities in Great Britain. And then, of course, there are the words of our own Scottish poet and tragedian William McGonagall who wrote a poem entitled 'The Beautiful City of Glasgow' which begins

> O, Beautiful City of Glasgow, which stands on the River Clyde,
> How happy should the people be, which in ye reside;
> Because it is the most enterprising City of the present day,
> Whatever anybody else may say.

and ends with the lines

> O, Beautiful City of Glasgow, I must conclude my lay,
> By calling thee the Greatest City of the present day,
> For your treatment of me was by no means churlish,
> Therefore I say, 'Let Glasgow Flourish'.

Appendix

Appendix 5

ORIGINS OF GLASGOW STREETS

Abbotsford Place – Was originally called Lawrie Street by James Lawrie who owned Laurieston in Gorbals. Later called Abbotsford, after the home of Sir Walter Scott in Roxburghshire.

Aikenhead Road – Leads to King's Park, which was once the Aikenhead Country Estate. For a period the estate was owned by Henry Erskine Gordon. This street was opened in 1802, and was built on his land. Aikenhead House within the park is being renovated at present in preparation to make it a costume museum.

The House was built in 1806 and designed by David Hamilton. The wings were added in 1823.

Albert Drive – Named after Prince Albert, husband of Queen Victoria. At No. 1 Albert Drive stands St Ninians Episcopal Church erected in 1872, the first Episcopal church to be built on the South Side of Glasgow.

Albion Street – Opened in 1808, built on church land, and for a period the site of a market for salt.

The name Albion was given to Britain by the Romans when they saw the white cliffs of Dover. The Latin for white is *Albus*.

Allison Street – Formed part of the original road from Paisley to Rutherglen and Hamilton. It is illustrated in a map of the Battle of Langside, 1568.

It perpetuates the name of Sir Archibald Alison, Bart., Sheriff of the County of Glasgow and author of *History of Europe*, who laid the foundation stone of Rutherglen Town Hall on 16th July, 1861.

Bell Street – Opened 1710. First called Bells' Wynd, then renamed after Sir John Bell, who was Provost of

Glasgow in 1680. He was a Royalist and was present at the Battle of Bothwell Bridge fought in 1679. His residence was in the Saltmarket on the south side of the Bridgegate.

Situated on an arch of the railway bridge at the corner of Bell Street and Spoutmouth is a plaque which states:–

Here stood
Davidson's Court
where the Spoutmouth Bible
Institute was
Founded in 1848.

Sir Michael Connal, born 1817, founded the institute. He was a merchant in Virginia Street, Glasgow. He was also one of the originators of the Glasgow Archaeological Society. In 1895 it was moved to 29 St Andrew's Square.

Berkeley Street – Named after Thomas Moreton Fitz-Hardinge, 6th Earl of Berkeley, (1796–1882). For a time the family owned Berkeley Square in London.

Blackfriars Street – Called after the Black Friars of the Order of St Dominic who wore a black cloak and hood. Friars are thought to have settled here around 1246.

Breadalbane Street – (Gaelic 'Brughad Albainn' meaning the breast or upland of Scotland). It lends its name to the Earl of Breadalbane. Breadalbane is in Perthshire in Clan Campbell Country.

Broomielaw – The first quay or jetty, complete with weigh-house and crane, was erected here in 1662. The street gets its name from a grassy slope or meadow covered with broom.

Bunhouse Road – Borrowed its name from the Bunhouse Grain Mill that stood in the vicinity.

Caledonia Road – A name derived from the Roman

word for the Kingdom of Scotland. The Roman General, Julius Agricola, first invaded Scotland in 80 A.D.

Camden Street – Named after the Marquis of Camden. The family seat is Bayham Abbey. The family own property in Camden Town in London.

All the original buildings in Camden Street are now gone. In their stead has been erected Blackfriars Primary School and residential flats.

Castle Street – Was the highway to the Bishop's Palace or Glasgow Castle depending on whether it was peacetime or wartime. Near here was the Howgate where executions took place in the 17th Century.

The Castle was demolished in 1792 to make way for the Royal Infirmary.

Cathcart Road – Is the highway to the district of that name.

Sir Herbert Maxwell, Bart. states that Cathcart in 1158 was written Kerkert, Cathair, or Caer Cairt, meaning the castle on the river.

The sturdy ruins of Cathcart Castle stood until 1980 beside Linn Park.

The White Cart flows through the district of Cathcart.

Cathcart Road in common with many other roads in Glasgow, has suffered greatly during the present redevelopment. It had a wide variety of small shops, which have now mostly been demolished.

Cathedral Square – Named after Glasgow Cathedral, surrounded by the Glasgow Cathedral, the Royal Infirmary, Provands Lordship, the oldest house in Glasgow, and the Ladywell and Drygate housing schemes, the latter built on the site of Duke Street Prison which was earlier known as the Stone Jug. In bygone days people convicted of witchcraft and heretics and Covenanters were hanged and burned here.

Cathedral Street – Built on the site of a narrow road

named Potter-Row Lone.

Charing Cross – Name taken from London, derived from Chere Reine Cross, so called from a memorial cross marking the site where the body of Eleanor, the Queen of Edward I was last set down while being carried to Westminster Abbey.

The cross was demolished by Puritans in 1647 and was later replaced by a new one.

Cheapside Street – Name borrowed from London. It was built on the site of a cheap market, hence the name.

Claremont Street – Was built on ground attached to Claremont House, which was formerly the site of the Botanic Gardens. It was named after a palace at Esher, Surrey, which was built by Lord Clive in 1768.

Cleland Street – Thought to be named after Lieutenant Colonel William Cleland, the first Colonel of the 26th Regiment, later the Cameronians or Scottish Rifles. He fought at Drumclog and was killed in an encounter at Dunkeld on 26th August, 1689.

Clyde Street – Was originally known as Horse Brae and on this site all kinds of quadrupeds were sold at fairs and markets. It runs adjacent to North Bank Walkway.

College Street – Was laid out by the Glasgow Corporation in 1794. It led to the old college, (founded 1451), in High Street.

The Albion Halls that stood at 29 College Street, were completely gutted by fire in 1909. The halls were used for union meetings, concerts and various other activities.

Coplaw Street – Built on the lands of Coplawhill, derived from the Scottish dialect 'cop' meaning cup, and 'law', a hill.

Craigie Street – Perpetuates the name of a village and parish near Kilmarnock in Kyle, Ayrshire.

Darnley Street – Named after a Barony in Eastwood,

Glasgow. It belonged to the house of Stewart. Sir John Stewart in 1488 became the Earl of Lennox. His fourth descendant, Henry Lord Darnley became the second husband of Mary Queen of Scots.

Derby Street – Named after Sir Frederick Stanley, 16th Earl of Derby (1841–1908) who was Governor General of Canada from 1888–93.

Douglas Street – Perpetuates the name of James Douglas of Mains who was left the estate of Mains by his grandfather and then took the name of Douglas although his name was originally Campbell.

Dover Street – Named after the town in Kent.

Many of the tenements in this street have now been demolished. Of its three churches, the church on the corner of Breadalbane Street and the Wesleyan Chapel at the corner of Claremont Street are gone as well, and the Kent Road Church of Scotland at the corner of Pembroke Street lies derelict. Dover Street and neighbouring streets once teemed with people and now lie stark and desolate.

Eglinton Street – Originally named Marlborough Street. Later renamed Eglinton Street after the Earl of Eglinton who was chairman of the Paisley and Johnstone Canal which ran adjacent to Eglinton Street.

The one-time Congregational Church at the corner of Devon Street and Eglinton Street was built in 1866. This date is cut deeply on the facade of the building. Since 1936 this has been a Christian Scientist Church. Strangely enough 1866 was the date that Christian Science was founded by Mary Baker Eddy. The Congregational Church moved to 161 Fenwick Road, Giffnock in 1936.

Elderslie Street – Takes its name from Elderslie in Renfrewshire, the birth place of Sir William Wallace, champion of Scotland's cause. Not a statue has been erected to him in this great city of Glasgow. Thomas

Campbell, the Glasgow poet wrote a dirge about him.

Elliot Street – The family name of the Earl of Minto. A member of the family was Governor General of India from 1806–14, another Governor General of Canada from 1898–1904, and another Viceroy of India from 1905–1910.

Lord Melgund of Minto House, Hawick, a descendant, accompanied Neil Armstrong, the astronaut, when he visited Langholm a few years ago to receive the freedom of that town.

Finnieston Street – Was laid out on the lands of Stobcross and was owned by John Orr of Barrowfield. It was named after Mr Finnie who was tutor to his family. Orr Street, Bridgeton, takes its name from this family.

Provost Patrick Colquhoun and Messrs Cookson of Newcastle opened the famous Verreville Pottery in 1777.

Gallowgate – Was laid out through the Gallowmuir, originally outside the Gallowgate Port.

Gorbals Street – (Gaelic 'Garbh-Ball' meaning a rough plot or piece of ground). Once known as St Ninians' Croft after a hospital built here in 1350. St Ninians Street, Gorbals, perpetuates the name.

William Quarrier (1829–1903) founder of Quarrier's Homes, who left his native town of Greenock with his family to come to Glasgow, first lived in Gorbals Street then known as Main Street.

The Talbot Centre for the homeless, the Citizens' Theatre, the old British Linen Bank and a clothing firm are the only buildings now left standing in Gorbals Street.

Grafton Square – Named after Augustus Henry Fitzroy, Duke of Grafton (1735–1811).

Granville Street – Carries the name of the Right Honourable Leveson Gower, K.G., Earl of Granville, 1815–91. He served under Sir William Ewart Gladstone, who has a statue in George Square.

Greendyke Street – Runs parallel to Glasgow Green from London Road to Saltmarket. The Green is the oldest park in Glasgow and once formed part of the Bishop's Forest.

High Street – Runs between Rottenrow and Glasgow Cross, one of the original streets of old Glasgow.

It led to the old Glasgow University and to the Bishop's Palace in Cathedral Square.

Howard Street – Formed in 1798, perpetuates the name of John Howard who was a famous philanthropist and brought about prison reform. This street is mostly formed on the site of the old Rope Walk that stood in this vicinity. The south side of Howard Street near Stockwell Street is the site of the old Town Hospital's graveyard. The hospital stood almost adjacent to the east side of Saint Andrew's Roman Catholic Cathedral in Clyde Street.

On the north side of Howard Street, stood St Enoch's Railway Station, St Enoch's Hotel and shops. They were demolished around 1977.

India Street – Glasgow had important trading links with the one-time Indian Empire.

Jamaica Street – Opened in 1763. It now leads to Glasgow Bridge. Three bridges have been built on this site.

Kent Road – Took its name from the property of George Sim, namely the villa called 'Kenthouse', which stood here.

The Mitchell Library has a new extension in Kent Road.

Kent Street – Opened in 1802, named after the Duke of Kent and formed on the Round Croft, belonging to Mr Struthers, a brewer. He had a penchant for English names, and named the other street on his land Suffolk Street.

Edward Irving, a popular preacher gave his name

to the Irvingites otherwise known as the Catholic Apostolic Church. He resided at 34 Kent Street.

Killermont Street – (From the Gaelic 'Coileir-Mointidh' meaning a neck or narrow piece of mossy land). Named after the lands of this name on the banks of the River Kelvin in the Parish of New Kilpatrick.

Ladywell Street – The name comes from a holy well or 'Well of Our Lady'. On the north side of the street is a niche in the wall of the Necropolis. The water became contaminated in consequence of its proximity to the cemetery and the well was closed.

Lancefield Street – Was built on the estate of that name. In 1821 David Napier, father of iron shipbuilding and marine engineering on the River Clyde, acquired the lands of Lancefield and built Lancefield House, Lancefield Docks and Lancefield Foundry.

Langside Road – Formerly Pathhead Road. It passed Pathhead Farmhouse at the top of the Granite Steps in Queen's Park on its way to old Langside Village situated where the Battle of Langside Memorial now stands in Battle Place. It was designed by Alexander Skirving in 1887. Skirving Street in Shawlands perpetuates his name.

Queen's Park United Free Church stood in this road near Queen's Drive. It was designed by Alexander Thomson, but on 25th March, 1943 it was destroyed by incendiary bombs during an air raid.

London Road – The first foundation stone for a building in this road, was laid by a deputation from the Trades Council in 1824.

The railway line extending from Stobcross Railway Station to Bridgeton Railway Station runs along underneath the full length of London Road.

A demolition worker stated that around 1957 a sandstone block was recovered from a demolished building in London Road near Rimsdale Street.

When it was broken up, it was found to contain a cannon ball.

MacNeil Street – Named after James MacNeil, who built it and who feued in 1818 part of the estate of Little Govan, now known as Polmadie, from Robert Houston Rae.

Three Covenanting martyrs were shot in Polmadie, namely Robert Thome, Thomas Cooke, and John Urie, by Major Balfour and Captain Metland. Their tomb dated 1685 is in Old Cathcart Churchyard.

Maitland Street – Built on the old Milton Estate and named after Helen Maitland Stirling.

Miller Street – Opened 1760 by Mr Miller of Westerton whose property it ran through.

Milton Street – Laid out on the estate of Milton. The family of Milton were related to the Stuarts of Castlemilk. Castlemilk was their home for nearly 600 years, as well as the House of Torrance, another family property in East Kilbride, Lanarkshire.

Both were taken over for building – one by the Glasgow Corporation around 1946 and the other by East Kilbride Council. Castlemilk is now one of the largest housing estates in Glasgow.

Moncur Street – Named after John Moncur, a Councillor. Thought to have been a Councillor for Carlton, he had a wood turning business at 23 Soho Street.

Monkland Street – Named after the ancient barony of Monkland in Lanarkshire, which also gave its name to the Monkland Canal that once passed through this area. The canal is now infilled in the Glasgow Sector and forms the Monkland Motorway the first phase of which was opened in 1975 by Bruce Millan, Secretary of State for Scotland.

Monteith Row – The first tenement in the row was built by John Mathieson, Manager to Henry Monteith & Co. of the Turkey Red Industry.

Montrose Street – Formed 1787. Named after the

Duke of this name.

Moray Place – Named after Regent Moray, half brother of Mary Queen of Scots. She was defeated by his forces at the Battle of Langside on 13th May, 1568. In this area memories are revived, of this episode in the names of streets, such as Queen's Drive, Queen Mary Avenue, Marywood Square, Regent Park Square and Queen's Park Avenue.

On the railway embankment of the now defunct Strathbungo Railway Station, facing Regent Park Square, are two sculptured stone heads, which were originally decorations for the old station.

Nairn Street – Called after the capital of Nairnshire. Nairn is derived from the Gaelic 'Uisge-Nearn' meaning river of alders.

Nithsdale Road – Named after the Maxwells' of Caerlaverock who were Earls of Nithsdale, a title now defunct.

North Hanover Street – Opened in 1787, named in honour of the House of Hanover, the title borne by the kings of Britain from 1714 till 1837. This street was previously named David Street.

North Street – Was originally named Lang Road and led north from the pretty little village of Anderston to the wooded heights above present Charing Cross. Later when the Woodside Mills were built in 1770, it was renamed Woodside Road. Finally it was renamed North Street in honour of Frederick North, son of Lord North who was Prime Minister in 1770.

The approach roads to the Kingston Bridge run along the east side of North Street. Prior to erection of the bridge all the buildings on the east side were demolished.

The main entrance to Charing Cross Station once faced North Street. It was found necessary to move it to its present position in Elmbank Gardens.

Overnewton Street – Formed on the estate of this

name which was owned by Walter Gibson, Provost of Glasgow in 1688. He was then the greatest merchant in Glasgow and possessed three large ships, which he used to trade with France, Spain, Sweden, Norway and the American colonies. He announced that anyone wishing to emigrate to the American colonies would be granted an assisted passage on one of his ships.

They sailed on 20th February, 1684, and the conditions were that an adult travelled for £5 steerage class, children between the ages of two and fourteen travelled for 50 shillings, and younger children travelled free of charge.

Seventy acres of land were granted to each on arrival, at a yearly rent of one penny per acre. Tradesmen were allowed to travel free, on condition that they served him for three years without pay, only receiving clothing and food. Later land was also granted to them. It is not on record if the scheme was successful. His town house was situated in the north-west corner of the Saltmarket and Gibson Wynd was also named after him.

Paisley Road – Used for centuries as the main road between Glasgow and Paisley. Over a century ago mainly country estates and farms lay between Glasgow and Paisley, such as Windmill Croft, Parkhouse Estate, Plantation Estate and Barshaw Estate.

Since then these places have been completely built over with houses and industrial premises, except Barshaw Estate, which is now a public park.

Parliamentary Road – A special Act of Parliament was required in order to build this road. It was built on the northern Parliamentary boundary of Glasgow. Hence the name.

Parkhouse Lane – Off Duke Street. Was previously the avenue that led to Parkhouse Estate situated at the foot of Drygate Street.

In 1773 John Findlay the owner possessed a malt barn and an attachment of 20 acres of land.

Pitt Street – Named in memory of William Pitt, British Statesman and P.M. (1759–1806).

Pollokshaws Road – The main road from the district of Gorbals to Pollokshaws. All streets and districts beginning with the word Pollok are built on the former country estate of the Maxwells of Pollok. Pollok House in Pollokshaws was their country seat.

The first sod was cut on 3rd May, 1978 in Pollok Estate, to mark the beginning of the erection of the building to house the Burrell Collection.

Portugal Street – It is thought that this street as well as Portugal Street in London are named in honour of Catherine Braganza, Queen of Charles II. Braganza was the name of the rulers of Portugal from 1640–1910.

The only building now left in this once populous street is St John's Roman Catholic Church.

Preston Street – Named after the market town of Lancashire. A battle was fought in Preston on 17th August, 1648 between the Parliamentarians and Royalists in which the latter suffered a severe defeat.

Royal Crescent – One of the earliest crescents to be built in the West End of Glasgow.

St Andrews Road – Named after St Andrew, the Patron Saint of Scotland.

He was a brother of Simon Peter and a fisherman at Bethsaida. He was tied to a cross in the form of an 'X' which has since been known as the Cross of St Andrew.

St George's Road – Named after the Patron Saint of England and Portugal. Legend has it that he slew a dragon and afterwards preached the gospel.

St James' Road – Thought to be called after St James the apostle who was one of the sons of Zebedee. This road once formed the eastern end of Dobbies Loan and was in part formerly a Roman road.

St Vincent Street – Commemorates the victory of John Jervis on February 15th, 1797 off Cape St Vincent. St Vincent, a Spaniard, was a Saint and Martyr. He was tortured to death in a prison in Valencia by the Roman Governor in 304.

Saracen Head Lane – Runs off the Gallowgate. It was built outside the Gallowgate Port, an ancient entrance to Glasgow. It was on this site that St Mungo's Chapel and burial ground lay. The Saracen Inn was built here in 1755.

The Inn was demolished on 17th March 1905 and on its site was built Saracenhead Building, demolished in 1977 down to first floor level. In the backcourt of the building was St Mungo's Well where St Mungo met St Columba of Iona.

The water was noted for its purity and abundance. The well is now closed. Saracen is taken from the Arabic 'Sharkeyn'. Crusaders referred to the Mohammedans by this name.

Shuttle Street – Was laid out on the lands of Shuttlefield. Prior to this it was named Greyfriars Wynd. The Friars had a monastery nearby granted by a charter in 1479 by King James III.

Stevenson Street – Named after Nathaniel Stevensor of Braidwood near Carluke, who was Provost of Calton in 1826. He was grandfather of the late husband of Madam Stuart Stevenson, daughter of the last Laird of Castlemilk and of Royal Scottish lineage.

Stobcross Street – Was built on the original avenue leading to Stobcross House. It takes its name from a wooden cross that stood at the junction of Finnieston Street and the main road leading from the Bishop's Palace or Glasgow Castle to Partick.

Stockwell Street – Takes its name from a well that stood in the street.

The Carrick Temperance Hotel built in the 17th

century stood here as well and was visited by Cameron of Locheil at the time of the '45 Rebellion and by Jenny Lind, the Swedish singer known as 'the Swedish Nightingale'.

During demolition in 1976 several items were discovered including a bottle of Glen Livet Whisky dated 1885. Also found were a love letter addressed to a girl staying at the hotel, a secret panel and a menu card of 1915 listing a 5 course meal costing 1/6d (7½p).

At the foot of Stockwell Street berthed on the Clyde near Albert Bridge is the old sailing vessel *Carrick* built in 1864 and now used by the R.N.V.R. Club.

Moodies Court lay behind the Carrick Hotel. It was entered from 31 Argyle Street. Probably the last two back to back tenements in the City of Glasgow were situated here. They were recently demolished to make way for the new Argyle Street Railway Station.

Trongate – Was first known as St Thenew's Gate. The name was changed when the Trongate weighing machine was established.

It is said that the first shoemakers shop was opened in 1749 by William Colquhoun to the west of the Tron Church.

St Enoch's Square was also named after St Thenew but the name changed through time to its present form.

St Thenew was the mother of Glasgow's Patron Saint Mungo.

Turnbull Street – Named after Bishop Turnbull who was granted a bull from Pope Nicholas V to found Glasgow University in 1451.

In the little graveyard of St Andrew's-by-the-Green Episcopal Church standing in this street, Alexander Jamieson has a stone to his memory. It speaks of the severe penalties suffered by the Episcopalians between 1746 and 1792.

Union Street – Was named Union Place until Gordon Street was opened in 1802. The first Unitarian Chapel in Glasgow was built in this street. At this period it was hoped that this street would develop into a good shopping centre, but this didn't happen. It was too far west of the city. The Central Railway Station stands partly in Union Street. It was built in 1879 and was the railway terminal for southbound trains of the Caledonian Railway Network. Originally the terminal station stood in Bridge Street and was known as Bridge Street Railway Station. It was found convenient to extend the railway lines across the River Clyde and build the present Central Station.

Victoria Road – This is one of the many thoroughfares in Glasgow named in honour of Queen Victoria.

Westercraigs Street – Formed on lands of that name.

Easter and Westercraigs bordered on the east side of the Necropolis which was then known as Firpark and extended east to the Kennyhill Estate from which Kennyhill Square takes its name.

The Necropolis is formed on part of the Westercraigs. Golfhill, Meadow Park, Craigpark, Dunchattan, Broompark and Whitehill are the names of streets in the district of Dennistoun, which were named after country estates that existed in this area in the 1820's.

Woodlands Road – Is formed on the northern fringe of the lands of that name.

The mansion of the estate was built by James MacNayr, L.L.D. It stood in the oval of Park Circus. MacNayr was a writer in Glasgow and in 1780 entered the Faculty of Procurators.

He was also first editor of the *Glasgow Herald* in 1802 for a brief period of 2 months. His house was known as 'MacNayr's Folly' as it was considered foolish to build it on such an out of the way place and crowning a hill.

The hill is now all covered with houses.

Woodside Crescent – Was first called Britannia Street
and appears under that name on a Post Office map of
1848.